Yerma
by Simon Stone
after Federico García Lorca

Her	**Billie Piper**	Production Manager	**Igor**
John	**Brendan Cowell**	Stage Manager	**Pippa Meyer**
Mary	**Charlotte Randle**	Deputy Stage Manager	**Sophie Rubenstei**
Victor	**John MacMillan**		
Helen	**Maureen Beattie**	Assistant Stage Managers	**Louise Quarterm**
Des	**Thalissa Teixeira**		**Ella Saunders**
		Costume Supervisor	**Catherine Kodic**
Direction	**Simon Stone**	Lighting Operator	**Nick Di Gravio**
Design	**Lizzie Clachan**	Sound Operator	**Joel Nasibitt**
Costumes	**Alice Babidge**	Sound No 2	**Tom Pickering**
Light	**James Farncombe**	Stage Crew/	
Music and Sound	**Stefan Gregory**	Automation Operator	**Sam Shuck**
Video	**Jack Henry James**	Stage Crew	**Rhodri Evans**
Casting	**Julia Horan CDG**		**Assad Jan,**
Associate Lighting Designer & Relight	**Nicki Brown**		**Tim Knight,**
			Ryan Smalley
Associate Director	**Kate Hewitt**	Wardrobe Manager	**Nicki Martin-Har**
Assistant Director	**Sophie Moniram**	Dresser	**Rianna Azoro**
		Dyeing and Breakdown	**Gabrielle Firth**

Special thanks to:
Aydin Huang-Miah, Elizabeth & Jamal Huang-Miah; Alexa McCall, Caroline & George McCall; Cualann O'Kelly, Siobhan O'Kelly; Kester Whitaker, Elgiva Field & Ian Whitaker

		Costume Maker	**Felicity Langthor**
		Scenic Drafting	**Nick Murray**
		Production Work Placement	**Sophie Slater**
Soprano	**Adey Grummet**		
Alto	**Belinda Sykes**	Set built by	**Weld-Fab Stage Engineering, Bower Wood, Cardiff Theatrica Services and You Vic Workshops**
		Lighting equipment supplied by	**Stage Electrics and White Light**
		Sound equipment supplied by	**Stage Sound Services**

The Young Vic 2017 season is generously supported by Garfield Weston Foundation, Genesis Foundation, The Richenthal Foundation, The Sackler Trust and an anonymous donor.

We would like to thank Copperfield Rehearsal Rooms SE1, Anya Sizer and Venessa Smith from The Bridge Centre, Dr Geetha Venkat at the Harley Street Fertility Clinic and Naoko Tagai

CAST

MAUREEN BEATTIE / Helen

Previous Young Vic: *Yerma* and *The Skin of Our Teeth*.

Theatre includes: *Right Now* (Ustinov/Bush/Traverse); John Gabriel Barclay (Oran Mor); *The Jennifer Tremblay Trilogy* (Stellar Quines/Edinburgh Festival); *Romeo and Juliet* (Rose, Kingston); *Cherry Orchard* (Royal Lyceum Edinburgh); *Noises Off* (Old Vic tour); *Nuclear War, No Quarter, Waiting Room Germany* (Royal Court); *Enquirer, 27* (National Theatre Scotland); The Masterbuilder (Chichester); *The Merry Wives of Windsor, Othello* (National Theatre); *This Wide Night* (Soho/Clean Break); *Ghosts, Acting Up* (Citizens); The Histories, *Richard III, Titus Andronicus, The Man Who Came To Dinner, Mary and Lizzie, King Lear, Macbeth, The Constant Couple* (RSC); Medea (Theatre Babel/Edinburgh Festival); *Rebecca* (UK tour); *Small Change, The Taming of the Shrew* (Sheffield Crucible); *The Deep Blue Sea* (Nottingham Playhouse); Candida (Plymouth/Salisbury); Hard to Get, The Widows of Clyth (Traverse); *Othello* (Lyric Hammersmith) and *Daisy Pulls It Off* (Gielgud).

Film includes: *Spores, The List* and *The Decoy Bride*.

Television includes: *Outlander* Series 2, *Doctor Who* Christmas Special 2014, *Vera, Moving On-Letting Go, Midsomer Murders, Doctors, Lewis, The Worst Week Of My Life, The Last Musketeer, City Central, A Wing and a Prayer, Ruffian Hearts, Taggart, The Long Roads, Bramwell, All Night Long, The Chief* and *Casualty*.

BRENDAN COWELL / John

Previous Young Vic: *Yerma* and *Life of Galileo*.

Other theatre includes: *The Wild Duck* (Barbican, UK tour, Vienna and Amsterdam tour); *Once in Royal David's City, Miss Julie* (Belvoir, Sydney); *The Dark Room* (nominated for Best Actor at the Sydney Theatre Awards, Company B); *True West, Dissident, Goes Without Saying* (Sydney Theatre Company) and *MEN* (Old Fitzroy).

Film includes: *The Current War, Last Cab to Darwin, Broke, Beneath Hill 60* (nominated for Best Actor in a Feature Film, Australian Film Institute Awards); *Noise* (winner of Best Actor in a Feature Film, Film Critics' Circle Awards).

Television includes: *Game of Thrones, Brock, The Let Down, The Outlaw Michael Howe* (also written and directed); *The Borgias* (Series 3) and *Love My Way* (nominated for Outstanding Performance by an Actor, ASTRA Awards, Most Popular TV Actor, Silver Logie Awards and Outstanding Actor in a Drama Series, TV Week Awards as well as contributing several episodes over three series).

Credits as a writer (UK) include: *Happy New* (Trafalgar Studios); *Rabbit* (Frantic Assembly UK tour); *The Slap* (nominated for a BAFTA and Emmy Award).

JOHN MACMILLAN/Victor

Previous Young Vic: *Yerma, The Member of the Wedding* and *In The Red and Brown Water*.

Theatre includes: *Killer* (Shoreditch Town Hall); *Hamlet* (The Almeida); *The Homecoming* (Trafalgar Studios); *Children's Children, The Last Days of Judas* (Almeida); *Cymbeline* (Cheek by Jowl World Tour); *Piranha Heights* (Soho); *Macbeth* (nominated for the Ian Charleson Award; Royal Exchange, Manchester) and *Hamlet* (nominated for the Ian Charleson Award; Donmar/ Broadway).

Film includes: *Fury, Maleficent, World War Z, The Dark Knight Rises, Hanna* and *Heartless*.

Television includes: *Back, Ordinary Lies, Carnage, The Windsors, Chewing Gum, Hoff the Record, Critical, New Tricks, Silk* Series 1-3, *Miranda Unwrapped, Sherlock Homes: The Blind Banker* and *Hustle*.

BILLIE PIPER/Her

Billie Piper won Best Actress at the Olivier Awards 2017 and the Natasha Richardson Award for Best Actress at the Evening Standard Theatre Awards 2016 for her performance in *Yerma*.

Previous theatre credits include: *Great Britain, The Effect* (Oliver nomination for Best Actress; National Theatre); *Reasons To Be Pretty* (Almeida) and *Treats* (Evening Standard Theatre Awards nomination for Best Actress; Garrick).

Her film work includes: *City of Tiny Lights, Animals United, Things to Do Before You're 30, The Calcium Kid* and *Spirit Trap*.

Television credits include: Showtime's *Penny Dreadful*, *Doctor Who*, *A Passionate Woman*, *The Shadow in the North*, *The Ruby in the Smoke*, *Much Ado About Nothing*, *True Love* and *Canterbury Tales: The Miller's Tale*, *Secret Diary of a Call Girl* and *Mansfield Park*.

CHARLOTTE RANDLE / Mary

Previous Young Vic: *Yerma*, *Public Enemy* and *King Lear* (also Liverpool Everyman).

Theatre includes: *Plastic* (Theatre Royal Bath); *Medea* (Almeida); *Deluge* (Hampstead); *Birdland, Muse and Poem – Open Court* (Royal Court); *The Lyons* (Menier Chocolate Factory); *The King's Speech* (Tour & West End); *Decade* (Headlong); *Lingua Franca* (Finborough/59E59, New York); *Love the Sinner, Mother Courage and her Children, Romeo and Juliet, Marat/ Sade* (National Theatre); *All About My Mother* (Old Vic); *Rabbit* (Old Red Lion/Trafalgar Studios/59E59, New York); *Don Carlos* (also West End); *Iphigenia, Sexual Perversity in Chicago, The Man Who Had All The Luck* (Sheffield Crucible); *Fuddy Meers* (Birmingham Rep/West End); *Lobby Hero* (Donmar Warehouse/ West End); *The Taming of the Shrew* and *The Dispute* (also Lyric Hammersmith) (RSC).

Film includes: *Being Considered, Joyride, The Honest Courtesan* and *The Token King*.

Television includes: *The Coroner; Father Brown, The Trials of Jimmy Rose, Silent Witness, Legacy, Holby City, Doctors, The Bill, Casualty, The IT Crowd, The Brides in the Bath, EastEnders, McCallum, The Miller's Tale* and *Lord Elgin*.

Radio includes: *The Gambler, The Other Man, Don Carlos* and *The Ideal Heroine*.

THALISSA TEIXEIRA / Des

Previous Young Vic: *Yerma*.

Theatre includes: *Othello, The Broken Heart, The Changeling* (Shakespeare's Globe); *The Night Watch* (Royal Exchange); *BU21* (Theatre 503) and *Electra* (Old Vic).

Film includes: *Takedown*.

Television includes: *The Musketeers* and *Midsomer Murders*.

CREATIVE TEAM

SIMON STONE / Direction

Previous Young Vic: *Yerma*.

Theatre includes: *Ibsenhuis* (Toneelgroep Amsterdam, Festival d'Avignon); *Husbands and Wives* (Toneelgroep Amsterdam); *Peer Gynt* (Neue Schauspielhaus, Hamburg); *Rocco und seine Brüder* (Munich Kammerspiele); *John Gabriel Borkman* (Burgtheater Vienna); *Thyestes* (Théâtre Nanterre-Amandiers, Paris, Belvoir Sydney & Malthouse Theatre Melbourne); *Drei Schwestern* (Theater Basel, Théâtre de l'Odéon, Paris); *Angels in America* (Theater Basel); *Medea* (Toneelgroep Amsterdam); *Die Orestie* (Theater Oberhausen) *The Government Inspector* (Belvoir Sydney & Malthouse Theatre Melbourne) *The Wild Duck* (winner of Helpmann and Sydney Theatre Awards 2010, Wiener Festwochen, Holland Festival, Barbican London, Perth Festival, Belvoir Sydney & Malthouse Theatre Melbourne); *Neighbourhood Watch* (Belvoir Sydney & Melbourne Theatre Company); *Miss Julie* (writer; Belvoir Sydney) *Hamlet* (Belvoir Sydney); *Cat on a Hot Tin Roof* (Belvoir Sydney); *The Cherry Orchard* (Melbourne Theatre Company); *Face to Face* (Sydney Theatre Company); *Death of a Salesman* (Belvoir Sydney); *Strange Interlude* (Belvoir Sydney); *Baal* (Sydney Theatre Company & Malthouse Theatre Melbourne). Founder & Artistic Director of The Hayloft Project, productions include *The Promise, The Only Child, The Suicide, Spring Awakening, B.C.,* and *Chekhov recut – Platonov*.

Opera includes: *Lear* (Salzburg Festival) and *Die Tote Stadt* (Theater Basel).

Film and short film include: *The Daughter* and *Reunion*.

LIZZIE CLACHAN / Design

Previous Young Vic includes: *Life of Galileo, Yerma, A Season in the Congo, The Girlfriend Experience* (and Royal Court) and *The Soldier's Fortune*.

Other theatre includes: *Gloria* (Hampstead); The *Suppliant Women* (ATC/Lyceum, Edinburgh & tour); *Three Sisters* (Theater Basel); *Winter Solstice* (Orange Tree Theatre); *Ibsen House* (Toneelgroep, Amsterdam); *The Truth* (Menier Chocolate Factory/Wyndham's); *The Invisible Hand* (Tricycle);

Cyprus Avenue (also Abbey Theatre, Dublin); *Fireworks, Woman and Scarecrow, Ladybird* (Royal Court); *Macbeth, As You Like It, The Beaux Stratagem, Treasure Island, Edward II, Port* and *A Woman Killed With Kindness* (National Theatre); *Tipping the Velvet* (Lyric, Hammersmith/Lyceum Edinburgh); *The Skriker* (MIF/Royal Exchange, Manchester); *Carmen Disruption* (Almeida); *The Forbidden Zone* (Salzburg / Berlin); *All My Sons* (Regent's Park Open Air Theatre); *Alder & Gibb, Gastronauts, The Witness, Jumpy* (also West End); *Our Private Life, Aunt Dan and Lemon, The Girlfriend Experience* (also at Plymouth Drum); *On Insomnia and Midnight, A Sorrow Beyond Dreams* (Burgtheater, Vienna); *Longing, The Trial of Ubu, Tiger Country* (Hampstead); *The Rings of Saturn* (Schauspiel Cologne); *Happy Days* (Sheffield Crucible, winner of Best Design at the Theatre Awards UK); *Far Away* (Bristol Old Vic); *Shoot/Get Treasure/Repeat* (Paines Plough); *I'll Be the Devil, Days of Significance* and *The American Pilot* (RSC).

Opera: *Pelleas and Melisande* (Grand Theatre Provence, Aix Festival); *Bliss* (Staatsoper Hamburg) and *Le Vin Herbe* (Staatsoper Berlin).

Lizzie co-founded Shunt in 1998 and designed all of their productions.

ALICE BABIDGE / Costumes

Alice designs set and costume in theatre, opera and film.

Theatre includes: Cat on a Hot Tin Roof (at Apollo); *Yerma* (Young Vic); *Three Sisters, The Lost Echo, The War of the Roses, Gross Und Klein, A Midsummer Nights Dream, All My Sons, King Lear, Suddenly Last Summer, Cyrano De Bergerac, Macbeth, The White Guard* (Sydney Theatre Company); *The Present* (Sydney Theatre Company and Barrymore Theatre, New York); *The Maids* (Sydney Theatre Company and Lincoln Centre, New York); *Waiting For Godot* (Sydney Theatre Company and Barbican); *Miss Julie, The Cherry Orchard* (MTC) and *The Oresteia* (Theatre Oberhausen).

Opera includes: *Hamlet* (Glyndebourne Festival); *Peer Gynt* (Deutsches SchauSpielHaus, Hamburg); *Der Ring Des Nibelungen, The Marriage Of Figaro* (Opera Australia); *Bliss* (Opera Australia and Edinburgh Festival); *Caligula (English*

National Opera and then Colon Theatre); *The Return Of Ulysses* (English National Opera and Young Vic); *Rigoletto* (Komische Oper Berlin) and *The Navigator* (Brisbane Festival and Melbourne International Arts Festival).

Film includes: *Holding The Man, Snowtown, Reunion, Red, Apricot, Castor And Pollux* and *Some Static Started*.

Television includes: *Hammer Bay*.

JAMES FARNCOMBE / Light

Previous Young Vic: *Yerma, Measure for Measure, The Cherry Orchard, Three Sisters, The Changeling* and *The Glass Menagerie*.

Theatre includes: *People, Places & Things* (also West End; Olivier nomination for Best Lighting Design); *Twelfth Night, The Plough and the Stars, Man and Superman, 3 Winters, Edward II, Men Should Weep, People, The Magistrate, London Road, Double Feature* (National Theatre); *White Devil, As You Like It, A Mad World My Masters* (RSC); *The Tempest, Henry IV* (St Ann's NYC); *Julius Caesar* (Donmar at King's Cross); *Anatomy of Suicide*, (Royal Court); *The Duchess of Malfi* (Old Vic); *The Dresser* (Duke of York's); *The Ladykillers* (also Geilgud); *Swallows and Amazons* (Vaudeville) and *Ibsen Huis, De Meiden* (ToneelGroep, Amsterdam).

Opera includes: *The Barber of Seville* (Glyndebourne); *Marriage of Figaro* (Opera North); *Pelléas et Mélisane* (Den Norske Opera); *Le Vin Herbé* (Berliner Staatsoper); *Ariodante* (Scottish Opera); *Pelléas et Melisánde, Alcina, Trauernacht* (Aix-en-Provence Festival) and *Benjamin, Dernière Nuit* (Opera de Lyon).

Ballet includes: *The Nutcracker, Carmen* and *Firebird* (Norwegian National Ballet, Oslo).

NICKI BROWN / Associate Lighting Designer & Relight

Nicki is Head of Lighting at the Young Vic.

Young Vic includes: *Cat on a Hot Tin Roof* (at Apollo Theatre); *A Midsummer Night's Dream, Yerma, A View from the Bridge, Happy Days* and *The Changeling* (all as Associate Lighting Designer); *Why It's Kicking Off Everywhere, Blackta, The Space Between, The Surplus, The Curtain, Two Endless Minutes* (all as Lighting Designer)

Other theatre includes: *Hedda Gabler* (NT); *Lazarus* (Kings Cross) (both as Associate Lighting Designer); *36 Phone Calls* (Hampstead); *A Miracle, Gone Too Far!, Contractions, Fear & Misery/War & Peace* (Royal Court); *93.2fm* (Royal Court and UK tour); *The Exquisite Corpse* (SouthwarkPlayhouse, Wales Millennium Centre); *The Duke in the Darkness* (Tabard); *8 Women* (Southwark Playhouse); *Gutter Junky* (Riverside Studios); *Ours* (Finborough); *By Parties Unknown* (site specific) and *The Elephant Man* (Union and Brazilian tour) (all as Lighting Designer); *Much Ado About Nothing* (Old Vic, as Assistant Lighting Designer).

STEFAN GREGORY / Sound

Stefan is an Australian-based composer and sound designer.

Previous Young Vic: *Yerma*.

Other theatre includes: *Husbands and Wives, Medea, Ibsen Huis* (Toneelgroep Amsterdam); *Engel In Amerika, Drei Schwestern* (Theater Basel); *The Wild Duck, Thyestes, Mother Courage and Her Children, The Glass Menagerie, Elektra/ Orestes, A Christmas Carol, The Government Inspector, Hamlet, Forget Me Not, Cat on a Hot Tin Roof, Peter Pan, Private Lives, Medea, Death of a Salesman, Old Man, Strange Interlude, B Street, As You Like It, The Seagull, Measure for Measure, That Face* (Belvoir St Theatre); *King Lear, The Present, Suddenly Last Summer, Face to Face, Dance Better At Parties, Baal, The War of the Roses* (Sydney Theatre Company); *Rocco und Seine Brüder* (Münchner Kammerspiel) and *The Cherry Orchard, Minnie and Liraz* (Melbourne Theatre Company).

Dance includes: *Puncture* (Sydney Philharmonia Choirs/Legs On The Wall); *Symphony* (Sydney Festival/Legs on the Wall); *L'Chaim!* (Sydney Dance Company) and *There Is Definitely a Prince Involved* (The Australian Ballet).

Stefan was a band member of Faker until 2008 and was awarded a Sidney Myer Creative Fellowship in 2014.

JACK HENRY JAMES / Video

Theatre includes: *Behind the Beautiful Forevers, Is There WIFI in Heaven?* (National Theatre); *After Miss Julie* (Theatre Royal Bath); *The Merchant of Venice, The Turn of the Screw* (Almeida); *In The Republic of Happiness, Tribes* (Royal Court); *Julius Caesar* (also St Ann's Warehouse, NYC); *Making Noise Quietly* (Donmar Warehouse); *Flare Path* (Theatre Royal Haymarket); *I Dreamed a Dream* (UK Tour); *Water Babies* (Leicester Curve); *Vampirette – The Musical* (Manchester Opera House); *Haunted* (Sydney Opera House Studio/59E59 NYC/UK Tour); *Chess the Musical* (UK Tour/Toronto); *The Lady From The Sea* (Manchester Royal Exchange); *Speaking in Tongues* (Duke Of Yorks, Associate); *42nd Street* (Chichester, as Animator); *Armstrong and Miller Live, Katy Brand's Big Ass Tour* (UK Tour, as Animator).

Opera includes: *Flight (Opera Holland Park).*

As a founding director of Really Creative Media Jack has worked all over the world with artists such as Queen, Goldfrapp and the Pet Shop Boys, and for fashion brands such as Versace and Anya Hindmarch.

JULIA HORAN CDG / Casting

Julia is an Associate Artist at the Young Vic.

Previous Young Vic: *Blue/Orange, The Trial, Ah, Wilderness!, Happy Days, Man: Three plays by Tennessee Williams, A View from the Bridge* (also Wyndham's/New York); *Public Enemy, The Shawl, Blackta, A Doll's House* (also Duke of York's/BAM); *After Miss Julie, The Government Inspector* and *The Events* (also ATC); *Wild Swans* (also ART).

Other theatre includes: *Harry Potter and the Cursed Child* (Palace); *Hamlet* (Barbican); *Uncle Vanya, Medea, Oresteia* (also Trafalgar Studios); *Game, Mr Burns, Chimerica* (also Harold Pinter); *Before the Party, King Lear, Children's Children, The Homecoming* (Almeida); *Hope, Teh Internet Is Serious Business, Wolf from the Door, The Nether* (also Duke of York's); *Adler and Gibb, Birdland, Khandan, The Mistress Contract, The Pass, Wastwater, Tribes, Clybourne Park* (also Wyndham's); *Spur of the Moment, Sucker Punch* (Royal Court); *The Lighthouse Keeper* (BCMG) and *Red Velvet* (Tricycle/St Ann's Warehouse/Garrick).

Film includes: *The Kaiser's Last Kiss* and *Departure.*

SOPHIE MONIRAM / Assistant Director

Previous Young Vic: *Yerma, Creditors* (both as Assistant Director) and *Noah* (short play, as Director).

Theatre as director includes: *Midsummer Roman Feast* (The RSC: Avonbank Gardens); *POT* (Ovalhouse, supported by Stratford Circus); *The Diary of a Hounslow Girl* (Ovalhouse, Southbank Centre and national tours with Black Theatre Live and House Theatre); *The Five Stages of Waiting* (Tristan Bates Theatre); *F**king Outside the Box* (VAULT Festival); *Creditors* (Cockpit); Indian Summer (White Bear); *Purgatorio, The Star-Spangled Girl* (Karamel Club) and *Zero Degrees* (Devised; Annex Theatre, Southampton).

Theatre as assistant director includes: *Myth* (The RSC: TOP); *The Rise and Shine of Comrade Fiasco* (Gate) and *As You Like It* (Cockpit Theatre & TIE Tour).

Sophie has also developed new writing for VAULT Festival and Edinburgh Festival, and directed rehearsed readings at Soho Theatre and at The National Theatre Studio.

About The Young Vic

Our shows
We present the widest variety of classics, new plays, forgotten works and music theatre. We tour and co-produce extensively within the UK and internationally.

Our artists
Our shows are created by some of the world's great theatre people alongside the most adventurous of the younger generation. This fusion makes the Young Vic one of the most exciting theatres in the world.

Our audience
…is famously the youngest and most diverse in London. We encourage those who don't think theatre is 'for them' to make it part of their lives. We give 10% of our tickets to schools and neighbours irrespective of box office demand, and keep prices low.

Our partners near at hand
Each year we engage with over 11,000 local people – individuals and groups of all kinds including schools and colleges – by exploring theatre on and off stage. From time to time we invite our neighbours to appear on our stage alongside professionals.

Our partners further away
By co-producing with leading theatre, opera, and dance companies from London and around the world we create shows neither partner could achieve alone.

'The hottest incubator of revitalized classics in London'
The New York Times

'The Young Vic is where theatre magic happens'
Time Out

'The best theatre in London'
The Telegraph

'London's most essential theatre'
The Guardian

'Young Vic is London's most lovable theatre. The building welcomes; the programming dares. It offers danger in a safe place'
The Observer

The Young Vic is a company limited by guarantee, registered in England No. 1188209.

VAT registration No. 236 673 348

The Young Vic (registered charity number 268876) receives public funding from:

Get more from the Young Vic online

 /youngvictheatre

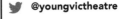 @youngvictheatre

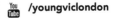 /youngviclondon

 youngviclondon.wordpress.com

/youngvictheatre

Sign up to receive email updates
at **youngvic.org/register**

Supporting The Young Vic

To produce our sell-out, award-winning shows and provide thousands of free activities through our Taking Part programme requires major investment. Find out how you can make a difference and get involved.

As an individual... become a Friend, donate to a special project, attend our unique gala events or remember the Young Vic in your will.

As a company... take advantage of our flexible memberships, exciting sponsorship opportunities, corporate workshops, CSR engagement and venue hire.

As a trust or foundation... support our innovative and forward-thinking programmes on stage and off.

Are you interested in events... hire a space in our award-winning building and we can work with you to create truly memorable workshops, conferences or parties.

For more information visit **youngvic.org/support us** **020 7922 2810** Registered charity (no. 268876)

BackstageTrust

Garfield Weston
FOUNDATION

phf Paul Hamlyn
Foundation

The Young Vic relies on the generous support of many individuals, trusts and foundations, and companies to produce our work, on and off stage. For their recent support we thank:

Public Funders
Arts Council England
Big Lottery Fund
British Council
Creative & Cultural Skills
Goethe-Institut
Lambeth Borough Council
Southwark Council

Corporate Partners
American Express
Barclays
Berkeley Group
Bloomberg
IHS Markit
Wahaca

Corporate Members
aka
Clifford Chance
Finsbury
Ingenious Media PLC
Memery Crystal
Royal Bank of Scotland and NatWest

Partners and Upper Circle
Anonymous
Lionel Barber & Victoria Greenwood
Sarah Billinghurst Solomon
Tony & Gisela Bloom
Simon & Sally Borrows
Sandra Cavlov
Caroline & Ian Cormack
Manfred & Lydia Gorvy
Patrick Handley
Jack & Linda Keenan
Adam Kenwright
Patrick McKenna
Simon & Midge Palley
Karl-Johan Persson
Barbara Reeves
Jon & NoraLee Sedmak
Dasha Shenkman
Rita & Paul Skinner

Bruno Wang
Soul Mates
Anonymous
David & Corinne Abbott
Clive Bannister
Chris & Frances Bates
Ginny & Humphrey Battcock
Anthony & Karen Beare
Joanne Beckett
Royce & Rotha Bell
Lady Primrose Bell
The Bickertons
Adrian & Lisa Binks
James Brimlow
Sarah Bunting
Eva Boenders & Scott Stevens
Beatrice Bondy
Katie Bradford
CJ & LM Braithwaite
Dr. Neil & Sarah Brener
Clive & Helena Butler
Roger & Alison De Haan
Annabel Duncan-Smith
Sean Egan
Jennifer & Jeff Eldredge
Sir Vernon and Lady Ellis
Don Ellwood & Sandra Johnigan
Ian & Margaret Frost
Jill & Jack Gerber
Sarah Hall
Katherine Hallgarten
Richard Hardman & Family
Frances Hellman and Warren Breslau
Nik Holttum & Helen Brannigan
Jane Horrocks
Mike and Caroline Howes
Linden Ife
Tom Keatinge
John Kennedy
John & Gerry Kinder
Ken & Mimi Lamb
Carol Lake

YERMA

Simon Stone

YERMA

after Federico García Lorca

OBERON BOOKS
LONDON

WWW.OBERONBOOKS.COM

First published in 2017 by Oberon Books Ltd
521 Caledonian Road, London N7 9RH
Tel: +44 (0) 20 7607 3637 / Fax: +44 (0) 20 7607 3629
e-mail: info@oberonbooks.com
www.oberonbooks.com

A catalogue record for this book is available from the British
Library.

PB ISBN: 9781786822635
E ISBN: 9781786822642

Cover image by Johan Persson

Printed and bound by 4edge Limited, Essex, UK.
eBook conversion by CPI Group (UK) Ltd, Croydon, CR0 4YY.

Visit www.oberonbooks.com to read more about all our books
and to buy them. You will also find features, author interviews and
news of any author events, and you can sign up for e-newsletters
so that you're always first to hear about our new releases.

Characters

HER

JOHN

MARY

VICTOR

HELEN

DES

1.1

JOHN: Hey stop hogging the Hawaiian.

HER: You hate Hawaiian.

JOHN: I told you it's always the lesbians.

HER: Whoever invented this must have had a cognitive disorder.

JOHN: Follow the lesbians.

HER: The what?

JOHN: Cognitive disorder?

HER: That's what you said. When we went on that date in Nolita. Don't you remember.

JOHN: Vaguely.

HER: Where are the keys?

JOHN: Somewhere on the floor.

HER: Here?

JOHN: Yeah somewhere. Do you want to hear my theory or not?

HER: This floor or the floor above? Or the basement?

JOHN: We have so many floors…

HER: We do… Go on then. Tell me your theory.

JOHN: Follow the lesbians.

HER: I heard you the first time.

JOHN: That's what the artists do. They follow the lesbians.

HER: Right.

JOHN: Any given suburb. First there's average working class. Then there's crack dealers. Then there's artists come buying from the crack dealers. Then they tell their gay friends about the wicked ass neighbourhood they've been buying their crack at and the gays are all fuck yeah I can't afford Dalston anymore anyhow but the male gays they're too pussy, don't want to get their Prada all messed up, but the chicks, they got something to prove, they're hard ass lesbian bitches, they come buy a two up two down, roll their sleeves up, get their hands dirty and…

HER: Lay the first stone of gentrification.

JOHN: That's what I'm talking about. Follow the lesbians.

HER: Are there still crack dealers here?

JOHN: Nobody deals crack anymore babe.

HER: You just said crack deal –

JOHN: Poetic license babe.

HER: Don't call me babe.

JOHN: Sugarnipples.

HER: Are there meth dealers or whatever I haven't heard of yet dealers?

JOHN: I'd imagine so.

HER: You think they'd mug me? Or, you know…

JOHN: Babes, you see what I did there, added an s to the end of it, babes –

HER: Oh my God.

JOHN: Listen babes, we are in the *safest* suburb in London. Where'd you think they mug people? Where they can get away with it. The muggers, they're fucking small fry. This is a fucking drug dealer's paradise right now. Police barely know it exists. It's just full of lesbians and whatever-dealers. You think they're gonna let that haven get violated by some fucking piddly mugger stealing three pounds from a right-on journalist girl who hasn't shaved her armpits since Kurt Cobain died?

HER: You like my armpits.

JOHN: I love your armpits.

HER: You don't like my armpits?

JOHN: It's how you're seen babes. By the world. Poetic brevity.

HER: Stop that. Stop joking.

JOHN: I'm serious.

HER: You hate my armpits?

JOHN: I love your chewbaccas.

HER: My what?

JOHN: Your little big-foots.

HER: Do they smell?

JOHN: A little. You know I think it's ironic that you're like a baby down there and up here you're like Mama Ginetta.

HER: Mama Ginetta. They smell?

JOHN: That's the first Italian woman's name I could think of.

HER: You're so fucking racist. I shave down *here* because you like it.

JOHN: I love it.

HER: But I'd never bloody admit it.

JOHN: God forbid that your compatriots at Free the Nipple would know you succumb to a man's desires.

HER: But armpits they see.

JOHN: Can't have that.

HER: You sure you didn't leave the keys in the door?

JOHN: Go check.

HER: I'm enjoying the champagne.

JOHN: *Veuve Clicquot.*

HER: Not *Dom Perignon.*

JOHN: We're not Dom yet babes.

HER: You want to fuck?

JOHN: On the floor?

HER: Where else?

JOHN: I'm a little tipsy.

9

HER: Why aren't we Dom yet?

JOHN: You want to buy that coffee table? We're not Dom. You want to buy those hanging planters, we're not –

HER: It's a beautiful coffee table.

JOHN: You write all those anti-materialistic blogs but really you're –

HER: Blog singular.

JOHN: Huh?

HER: I have one blog. Not blogs. I post posts.

JOHN: Whatevs.

HER: You're in a funny mood.

JOHN: I'm learning the lingo. Whatevs babes. Lol.

HER: Can we afford the coffee table?

JOHN: We're not Dom.

HER: Maybe we should consider Art Deco, it's clean, pure lines, but not so in right now.

JOHN: Whatever you say.

HER: Art Deco. The chairs are blockier. And the coffee tables. Maybe French provincial.

JOHN: That is an issue with Art Deco… We'll get a nice coffee table.

HER: Fucking eBay. What did we just do?

JOHN: Oh I don't know… Just a little purchaiise.

HER: We just bought a house didn't we?

JOHN: It's not in Marylebone don't worry hon, you've still got some outsider cred.

HER: No one who possesses a property has outsider cred.

JOHN: Especially not three floors.

HER: It is the middle of nowhere.

JOHN: Keep us fit.

HER: It took me less than an hour on the bike.

JOHN: You ride like a granny.

HER: Give me some more bike lanes Sadiq and I'll give you less granny.

JOHN: That worked out well didn't it?

HER: The house?

JOHN: Sadiq.

HER: I miss Boris.

JOHN: Shut the fuck up.

They laugh.

HER: Sure you don't want to fuck?

JOHN: I didn't say no. Just let me sober up first.

HER: You never want to fuck anymore.

JOHN: That's not true. And since when did we stop calling it making love?

HER: Since you got into the whole anal thing.

JOHN: Touché.

HER: Should I be more whorey in bed?

JOHN: What? Huh? No. No. You're exactly the right degree of whore.

HER: Why are you suddenly into bum sex?

JOHN: I've been…

HER: What?

JOHN: Stop it.

HER: No tell me.

JOHN: I've been watching some stuff and –

HER: I know.

JOHN: Wait. How do you know?

HER: You left the pages open on the laptop.

JOHN: I didn't close them?

HER: Maybe you fell asleep and forgot.

JOHN: Sorry babe. Bum sex?

HER: Bum sex.

JOHN: That's not very sexy.

HER: That's what it is. Sex in the bum.

JOHN: Jesus. Stop it.

HER: Do you prefer watching it? To doing it?

JOHN: What? Huh? No. It's just when you're home late. I can't go to sleep otherwise.

HER: Is it better?

JOHN: What?

HER: You know…

JOHN: What?

HER: The orgasm? When you're…

JOHN: No. Maybe. Sometimes. But it's me that's doing it. A connoisseur.

HER: A connoisseur of his own cock.

JOHN: This is getting smutty. Let's change the topic.

HER: What to?

JOHN: I don't know.

HER: Why does it irritate you so much talking about this stuff?

JOHN: It doesn't. I'm being completely honest. Like we agreed.

HER: Thank you. You're right.

JOHN: I'm sorry you had to see my YouPorn pages.

HER: That's alright darling. But maybe you could try cutting back.

JOHN: I could do that. I could. I could go cold turkey.

HER: Oh yeah?

JOHN: For my woman. Anything.

HER: We just bought a house.

JOHN: We did.

HER: Hey.

JOHN: Yeah?

HER: Hey you.

JOHN: Yeah?

HER: There's um…

JOHN: What?

HER: I'm embarrassed.

JOHN: *You're* embarrassed?

HER: No, no. Something else.

JOHN: What?

HER: Well we've got three floors right. Plenty of room…

JOHN: Yeah.

HER: Room for a children's bedroom. Room for two.

JOHN: Um…what?

HER: You heard me.

JOHN: What?

HER: Don't make me repeat it.

JOHN: I feel like I have to because my ears aren't believing it.

HER: Hon.

JOHN: Yes.

HER: I've been thinking.

JOHN: Clearly.

HER: And what I thought was. Well.

JOHN: Uh huh?

HER: I'm thirty-three.

JOHN: Are you? Shit. Where's my young assistant?

HER: Fuck off.

He laughs.

HER: And well…maybe it's not the stupidest idea.

JOHN: You hate babies.

HER: Well they're stupid aren't they? And completely self-centred. Like a retarded cat.

JOHN: Charming.

HER: I know. I know. But it's just that…

JOHN: What?

HER: Regret.

JOHN: About what?

HER: Not yet. But later maybe.

JOHN: Okay.

HER: And. Maybe, you and I …two smart, open-minded, liberal, caring individuals, with an awareness of our duty to the less fortunate, maybe it's exactly us that should be…

JOHN: Procreating?

HER: No. But yes.

JOHN: Our social duty so to speak.

HER: You don't think it's a good idea?

JOHN: I'm not saying that.

HER: You don't want to.

JOHN: I'm definitely not saying that.

HER: So do you want to?

JOHN: You want me to sign somewhere?

HER: We could infiltrate the bastards with a left-wing saboteur or two.

JOHN: Bring the system down from the inside. One foetus at a time.

HER: Shut up. I'm trying to be honest.

JOHN: I know hon.

HER: It's not who I am. I am not my reproductive system.

JOHN: I know that.

HER: That's not what you thought back then.

JOHN: Back then I wanted to conquer every last part of your reproductive system.

HER: And read T.S. Eliot to me at three in the morning.

JOHN: Why did I choose Eliot? Bukowski's so much cooler. But you can't blame me. It's my animal urge.

HER: Your animal urge is to spread your seed as far and wide as you can.

JOHN: No I'm like one of those penguins. Which one is it? The King or something?

HER: Huh?

JOHN: Or like a duck? Mate for life.

HER: Then why don't you want to fuck me?

JOHN: I do. Always.

HER: Not always.

JOHN: I'm in my early forties.

HER: Enough excuses.

JOHN: Hang on. Stop for a second. Are you serious?

HER: Of course I am.

JOHN: Then let's do it. Where is it?

HER: Where's what?

JOHN: The fucking pill. Where is it? Here?

Looks through her handbag.

HER: Hey that's my private property.

JOHN: I could sneak through it while you sleep.

HER: Do you? Is that what you do?

JOHN: Only to look for texts from strangers.

HER: Luckily I'm pathetically faithful.

JOHN: Me too. It's pathetic.

HER: Give it here.

JOHN: It's like fucking Mary Poppins in here.

HER: Give it here. There.

JOHN: Watch this.

He crushes her pills underfoot, one by one.

JOHN: It's meant to be a symbolic gesture destroying your contraception. But I didn't account for the texture of the carpet.

HER: Oh. That's kind of sexy.

JOHN: It is isn't it?

JOHN: To the future.

HER: To the future.

He downs the rest of the champagne.

JOHN: Next time we're buying Dom.

HER: Okay boss.

JOHN: Don't call me that.

HER: Why not? Nobody can hear. And we both know who's really the boss.

JOHN: Yes we do.

HER: Now let's fuck.

1.2

MARY: Take a break?

HER: No, it's almost done.

MARY: Those boys weren't half fit, eh?

HER: Boys?

MARY: The movers.

HER: Oh. I didn't notice.

MARY: Y'alright?

HER: Nothing. It's nothing.

MARY: His flight was delayed.

HER: I know. It's just.

MARY: The first night.

HER: Yeah.

MARY: Yeah.

MARY: You want me to stay over?

HER: No that's alright. He said there's a flight that gets him in early.

HELEN: We should check this place for woodworm.

HER: Give it a rest Mum.

HELEN: Plenty of room for kids, eh?

MARY: Mum…

HER: Well, yeah. Maybe.

HELEN: Excuse me what? What did you just? What did she just say?

MARY: Mum…

HER: I don't know. I've been thinking about it a bit.

MARY: Look at her she's grinning.

HELEN: And what? What's so wrong with that? Ever since your dad died…

17

MARY: Here we go…

HER: Mum…

HELEN: Don't. Don't do that. Treat me like a child.

MARY: We're not Mum…

HELEN: I'd given up hoping. I mean your sister here.

MARY: Fuck off Mum.

HELEN: Am I wrong?

HER: What? What's happened?

HELEN: He's been stepping out.

MARY: Mum.

HER: What?

MARY: It's none of your bloody business.

HELEN: And every other week there's another revelation.

HER: What? Hang on. Stop. What's going on? Why didn't you call me?

MARY: I did call you. You never answered.

HER: I what, sorry? What? Did you call from work it's always unknown when you –

MARY: Let's forget about it.

HER: I never answer unknown numbers.

HELEN: Anyway they're racking up.

MARY: MUM.

HELEN: You don't need him, love. Believe me, better alone than lonely.

MARY: Stop it with your fucking epigrams Mum, it's *complicated*. *Complicated*. Okay. We can't all be first wave feminists –

HELEN: Or any of the other waves.

HER: Give her a break Mum.

18

HELEN: Have you ever cheated on him?

MARY: Well no. Yes. Not exactly. I tried.

HELEN: *You tried?*

MARY: You know how weird it is to touch another man…after all those years…a stranger…

HELEN: He doesn't seem to be having any trouble with it.

MARY: MUM.

HER: Why haven't you told me anything about this?

HELEN: You're never there love. It's okay but –

HER: I'm there. Of course I'm there. Aren't I?

MARY: Well, to be honest…

HELEN: You're not love.

HER: Okay well, aren't I the asshole then?

MARY: No, I'm not saying that.

HELEN: She's not. But you are.

HER: Thanks Mum.

HELEN: The asshole…of our family group.

MARY: You want us to unpack these?

HER: No. Stop. Let's rewind a second. How long has this been going on?

HELEN: *Years.*

MARY: Shut the fuck up Mum.

HER: Yeah Mum shut the fuck up.

HELEN: How I managed to bring up two such disrespectful –

MARY: You know every since the accident he's been so…

HER: Yeah…

MARY: Yeah and he was drinking a lot more than I realised. I found a stockpile in the shed out the back. I mean none of us can imagine what it's like to be in constant pain.

HELEN: Oh God classic Stockholm Syndrome.

MARY: He can't work, he can't stay in one position for more than ten minutes so we can't go to the cinema together or on any dates at all really and he's drunk by the time I get home from work.

HELEN: And yet he still manages to find the energy to bed half of Camden Town.

MARY: It's more complicated than that Mum.

HELEN: Can't stay in one position for more than ten minutes? Must be very exciting for the lasses.

MARY: Well we're going to have to figure it out one way or the other now because things have progressed beyond the point of…

HER: What?

MARY: I think I'm…

HER: Oh…

HELEN: What's that? What's she saying?

MARY: In fact I know I'm…

HER: How long…

MARY: Two months.

HELEN: & HER: Oh. Oh my God.

MARY: Mum…

HER: Had you been trying?

MARY: No. Not at all. I mean, God, the way things are at the moment it was the last thing on my mind.

HER: But you were having a lot of…

MARY: No, not at all. I was on the pill.

HER: On the pill? Really? I mean is that even –

MARY: Yes it is.

HER: Right.

HELEN: Well this is a surprise.

1.3

JOHN: Did you miss me?

HER: Of course I did. I just moved into our house all on my own.

JOHN: I'm sorry babes.

HER: Don't say that. Don't call me that. I'm serious.

JOHN: Me too. I'm sorry. I shouldn't have left it so late. Barry organised us a meeting with the financiers at the last minute and it's a once in a lifetime –

HER: I'm happy for you.

JOHN: Are you? You don't sound like it.

HER: I am. Look at me I'm smiling.

JOHN: No you're not.

HER: Mary's pregnant.

JOHN: Mary's pregnant?

HER: Yes.

JOHN: Your sister? Mary?

HER: Yes.

JOHN: Whose husband never fucks her?

HER: He does. More than we do.

JOHN: Hey. Don't say that.

HER: It's true. I mean how am I ever going to get pregnant if you're away all the time?

JOHN: Hey. Hey. Slow down. Let's not put pressure on this.

HER: We decided months ago and we've barely even got started.

JOHN: Got started?

HER: You know what I'm saying.

JOHN: You want to do it now?

HER: No there's no point. I'm at the totally wrong end of my cycle.

21

JOHN: No point at all?

HER: I wouldn't want to waste the…

JOHN: The what?

HER: The I don't know. You tell me? The curiosity?

JOHN: I'm always curious.

HER: You know everything. You've seen everything. I should have been one of those Italian wives from the sixties who always turns the lights off –

JOHN: I like keeping the lights on.

HER: Is that why you always have a pillow over your head?

JOHN: I'm not trying to not –

HER: What then?

JOHN: I don't know I'm –

HER: You're bored of me.

JOHN: Whoa. Put the brakes on, this is getting way too –

HER: What are you doing then?

JOHN: I don't know I'm… I'm role-playing in my head.

HER: Role-playing? Imagining someone else? Someone from one of your pornos?

JOHN: No it's you.

HER: Someone from work? Someone you've seen on the tube?

JOHN: No. No. You.

HER: Me? I'm right in front of you.

JOHN: Yeah but…

HER: What?

JOHN: You as like a…

HER: What?

JOHN: Jesus stop looking at me like that.

HER: Me as what?

JOHN: I don't know. A cleaning lady who's walked in and found me naked.

HER: Fucking hell.

JOHN: You asked me. I told you. You want to hear the truth. That's the truth. It's always you but…

HER: But someone else?

JOHN: No. Different scenarios. Just to keep things. The mystery. You know.

HER: No I don't know. Because I don't imagine anyone else. I look at you and I get turned on. And I think about fucking you while I'm at work and when you're gone for three weeks when I masturbate, which I rarely do unless we're on Skype because I want to save it for you, I'm thinking of you. You. Not you as a fucking plumber.

JOHN: Alright fine. I'm sorry. I'll stop closing my eyes or… whatever… I'll look at you… This is really fucking turning me on analysing it like this.

JOHN: What is so wrong with talking about this problem?

JOHN: BECAUSE …sorry… Because there is no fucking problem. There is no problem. There is no problem. Okay?

…

JOHN: Right so now you're not going to talk to me for two days?

…

JOHN: I just landed one of the biggest contracts of my career. Everything is changing for me. We should be bathing in Dom Perignon. And this is what I come home to.

HER: You come home to a completely furnished, perfect house. Fuck you.

JOHN: And I can't thank you enough for that. It looks amazing. Please. Hey. Hey.

HER: Fuck off.

JOHN: You don't mean that.

HER: No.

JOHN: No. You don't.

HER: Don't fuck off.

JOHN: I won't. What's this app thing?

HER: It gives me alerts. When I'm most fertile.

JOHN: Okay.

HER: And that's when when we really need to…

JOHN: Jesus.

HER: WHAT?

JOHN: Two years ago you'd make me wear a condom, even when you were on the pill. To make double sure. And now you're like… what? Should we get our calendars out and make sure I'm always in town when your eggs are ready?

HER: Well what's so stupid about that?

JOHN: Okay.

HER: What?

JOHN: I'm gonna get an early night

HER: Where are you going?

JOHN: I'm knackered from the plane.

HER: John?

JOHN: I love you.

1.4

HER: Well that is…

VICTOR: I know…

HER: That is…

VICTOR: Surprise.

She laughs.

HER: Who the hell hired you?

VICTOR: Fiona. I thought you knew.

HER: I had no idea.

VICTOR: So it wasn't you pulling strings?

HER: No. You must have got it on your own merit.

VICTOR: There's a first for everything. How are you?

HER: Good. Great. You know. You? God. Exactly the same.

VICTOR: Really?

HER: Totally.

VICTOR: So what's been happening?

She laughs.

VICTOR: You married?

HER: God no. No.

VICTOR: Right.

HER: No way. God no. I'm still with –

VICTOR: Oh right?

HER: Yeah. Yeah.

VICTOR: Well that's…

HER: What?

VICTOR: Good, right?

HER: Well you know long term relationships…

VICTOR: Do I?

HER: Don't you?

VICTOR: Can't say so.

HER: No momentous love affairs?

VICTOR: Depends on your definition of momentous. No. I've had. Yeah. Sure. I think I'm quite difficult to manage.

HER: Manage?

VICTOR: Put up with.

HER: Oh what's so annoying about you?

He laughs.

HER: Sorry.

VICTOR: No. No. How's John?

HER: He's good. He's busy. Away a lot.

VICTOR: How's that?

HER: Great.

VICTOR: Yeah?

HER: Yeah. I like the space.

VICTOR: Watch whatever you want on Netflix.

HER: Haha. Yeah.

VICTOR: What's it been? Ten years?

HER: Has it? God.

VICTOR: I think so. Almost.

HER: Have I changed?

VICTOR: A little.

HER: You're supposed to say no. I told you you hadn't changed.

VICTOR: Yeah but you were lying.

HER: Is it shocking? Is it that bad?

VICTOR: What?

HER: Was it like a shock? Seeing the difference?

VICTOR: Hey…

HER: Was it like sad? I mean like depressing? Like Marlon Brando in the nineties?

VICTOR: Nothing like that.

HER: No?

VICTOR: No, more like Bette Davis in *Whatever Happened To Baby Jane*.

HER: God.

VICTOR: You look great.

HER: Thanks. You too.

VICTOR: And you're my boss.

HER: Shit. Yeah, I guess this constitutes workplace harassment.

VICTOR: Don't worry I won't tell. Senior editor for Life Style and Culture. Big ups. How did that happen so fast?

HER: Yeah a few of the right people died.

VICTOR: Did you put a hit out on them?

HER: What desk are you even on?

VICTOR: What do you think? Same old, same old? Politics. And you had any – ?

HER: Oh yeah, no, working on it.

VICTOR: Probably the right time about now isn't it?

HER: Yeah. Yeah. I thought I might give it a whirl.

VICTOR: Yeah I got a two-year-old myself.

HER: Oh.

VICTOR: Yeah. Yeah. Mistake really but…

HER: Mistake?

VICTOR: Well you know the circumstances of conception. Anything but a mistake now he's here.

HER: Are you still with the –

VICTOR: No, less than six months –

HER: Oh well that's –

VICTOR: Like I said, difficult to manage.

HER: Jesus you must be a nightmare.

VICTOR: Guess so.

HER: And you see each other –

VICTOR: Fifty fifty.

HER: Wow that's…

VICTOR: That's why I moved back here.

HER: Well if I get my skates on they can play with each other.

VICTOR: Skates on?

HER: I mean the age difference won't be too –

VICTOR: Oh yeah. Skates on. Well better tell John to lift his game.

HER: It's not. I don't think that's. Why. I mean we have…

VICTOR: Of course, sorry, joke.

HER: Right of course yeah. Haha.

VICTOR: This is going to sound weird and inappropriate probably.
So just tell me to stop if I …

HER: What?

VICTOR: I thought a lot about, well, you know, since then, and… I
still can't quite figure out what happened there, maybe not what but how
exactly and what I … Yeah, I just, regret what…and I'm happy for you
and think it's just great that you're still with John and that's going so well
but I just, is that okay? Just that it was well yeah, significant and yeah,
thought a lot about it…

1.5

HER: Have you seen this? It's only had fifty hits today.

DES: What?

HER: The blog. My blog.

DES: Oh. Yeah. Sorry.

HER: What the hell is happening? We're going to lose all of our adverts.

DES: Look how sunny it is. Everyone's probably in the park.

HER: You can still read blogs in the park.

DES: Doesn't that kind of defeat the purpose of going to the park?

HER: Oh please let's not start with that. People have always read books in the park, newspapers and now it's a… Your whole generation was born with an iPhone attached to your hand and now you're all, let's make moccasins by hand and brew our own vodka and travel across the Caucasus by horse-drawn cart.

DES: I just like parks.

HER: This fashionable slowness you're all into but you all freak out when you lose your 4G.

DES: Can I be honest with you?

HER: Of course you can you don't have to ask that.

DES: It's the pregnancy thing. The attempted pregnancy thing

HER: The attempted pregnancy thing?

DES: It's kind of splitting your demographic. I mean it's kind of killing your demographic. I mean it's cancerous to your demographic. I mean your brand… I know that a very commercial way of putting it but –

HER: Just –

DES: Yeah well your brand, why people buy your product…read your blog…

HER: Yeah?

DES: It's always been…they recognise it as…you used to be more political.

HER: I'm still political.

DES: It's like as if Lena Dunham started dating Donald Trump and talking about juice detoxes all the time. I mean, do you wanna watch that show? HBO would not commission that show.

HER: Like I said I appreciate your honesty but fuck off. Oh my God. Is it that bad?

DES: It's just a bit...nice... It's...sickeningly nice.

HER: Nice sells.

DES: Yeah well maybe you should write for Women's Health instead. Oh fuck.

HER: What?

DES: Oh fuck. I think I had sex last night.

HER: What do you mean you think you had sex last night?

DES: I can't remember.

HER: You can't remember?

DES: Yeah all I remember is tequila shots...and a Portuguese Uber driver and...

HER: You slept with an Uber driver?

DES: No we spoke Portuguese that's why I remember, no I can't remember who was next to me in the back but I think we were kissing.

HER: Does it feel like you had sex?

DES: Um...maybe?

HER: Who could it have been?

DES: Well any one of the about ten good-looking men that were at the party last night.

HER: Any one of the them? That's confident.

DES: God I hope it wasn't Henry. What I do? Do I just wait for someone to text? I should get the morning after pill.

HER: Why do you hope it wasn't Henry? Why aren't you on the pill?

DES: Because he's my best friend's boyfriend. No it fucks with my whole aura.

HER: What about the coil?

DES: Eugh.

HER: How often do you take the morning after pill?

DES: I don't know. Every now and then?

HER: Every now and then? Jesus. You're going to kill your uterus.

DES: I have every right to kill my uterus.

HER: You do. Yeah. Of course you do. But. A later version of you might. You know.

DES: I'll deal with it then.

HER: That's what I thought.

DES: See this is the kind of stuff you should have on the blog. The ugly stuff. The regrets. The nighttime horrors. What if I've ruined my womb? Maybe I shouldn't have had that abortion back then...

HER: Wait sorry. How do you know about the...

DES: Oh shit. Sorry.

HER: Oh right. You didn't.

DES: No.

HER: And I just.

DES: Yep.

HER: Well...yeah... I did have an abortion...

DES: Hey. I was looking through your drafts folder and – is that okay?

HER: It's fine it's you can yeah –

DES: And that bit about when your sister got pregnant and you couldn't stop crying and you found yourself consoling yourself with the thought that one in four pregnancies end in miscarriage –

HER: Oh God. I thought that for a split-second. It wasn't even me thinking it.

DES: Can you tell the difference?

HER: I just write everything down when I take notes I just spew.

DES: That's what works.

HER: Me vomiting on the internet?

DES: Yeah. The bit before the censorship.

HER: Journalism is more than that, you know that, otherwise I might as well just be updating my Facebook status.

DES: Of course yeah deconstruct the thought, explore it, the politics versus the biological impulse –

HER: Jesus I feel like I'm getting coaching from a twenty-year-old.

DES: I'm twenty-one.

HER: Is my blog really that boring?

DES: Yes.

HER: So what you want more descriptions of speculums in my vagina?

DES: YES. Why not? I mean if I was someone out there going through what you're going through –

HER: I'm not going through anything –

DES: Whatever you might be going through.

HER: It's perfectly normal for it to take a while to –

DES: Or not normal. Sometimes… That's the cliff-hanger.

HER: Jesus this is a great chat.

DES: Why else make it the focus of your blog?

HER: That's not why I –

DES: Well maybe that's what you need to figure out. You never pulled any punches before.

HER: Total honesty.

DES: Total sacrifice.

HER: Fuck you.

DES: Fuck you.

HER: Let's get back to work we are going to miss our deadline. Hey, did you organize that meeting with the Google people. They're totally fucking us on our search ranking. We're the second most important paper in the country.

A message comes through on phone.

DES: Oh wait. Hang on.

HER: Is it from the…

DES: Okay so I definitely had sex last night. You need anything from the chemist?

1.6

HELEN: I hated the idea of getting pregnant. Being colonised by someone's sperm. Eugh. You know that film *Alien*? Well that's a very accurate representation of what my pregnancies felt like. Waiting, horrified, feeling this creature growing inside me, until the day where it forced itself out of me, screaming demandingly, expecting me to satisfy its every whim, a parasitic succubus –

HER: Okay Mum. Thanks.

HELEN: Isn't this the kind of thing you want? Is the thingy still recording?

HER: Yes it is. And yes it is.

HELEN: Are you sure? I can't see a light.

HER: It's my phone the display's gone to sleep.

HELEN: But maybe it's died.

HER: No it's just – I do this all the time Mum – see it's still going.

HELEN: That was good that last bit. Succubus. Not often you get an opportunity to use that word.

HER: I just want you to talk naturally. Off the cuff.

HELEN: That is me off the cuff. That's how I talk.

HER: Okay great.

HELEN: What's next? You want to order some food?

HER: I'm not hungry.

HELEN: Maybe you're anorexic.

HER: I'm not.

HELEN: But maybe that's it. Maybe that's why. Oh my God were you anorexic and I didn't even notice?

HER: No I wasn't.

HELEN: That's a very common cause of infertility.

HER: I'm not infert – and yes I know Mum. I'm currently writing an exhaustive series of articles about these very topics.

HELEN: Oh you've already got the anorexia angle.

HER: Yes. Mum. Do you ever read my blog?

HELEN: No I'm far too busy. I've started on this Deliveroo thing. It's very handy. Do you know what that is? Deliveroo?

HER: Yes Mum. I know what Deliveroo is.

HELEN: You just get the app up see? And then you click on a restaurant see? Chinese, Turkish, Pakistani, Thai, you want Thai?

HER: I know Mum. I know what it is.

HELEN: See all the different options? Isn't that incredible? Takes twenty minutes. And you know exactly how far away the bike, or sometimes it's a scooter, how far away the scooter is. Isn't that incredible?

HER: Yes Mum.

HELEN: Sometimes I order things I don't even need. At eleven o'clock at night. And then I've got half a peking duck and I don't know what to do with it. Isn't that bizarre? Maybe I've got dementia.

HER: Why did you never hold me?

HELEN: What?

HER: When I was a child. When we were children. Why didn't you hold us?

HELEN: What are you going about? Of course I held you.

HER: You didn't. Except that time I fell off the bike and knocked out my two front teeth. I remember thinking oh that feels nice. And I looked up at you and you looked very uncomfortable. Patting me awkwardly like you'd pat a stranger's dog.

HELEN: This is nonsense. Why are you making this stuff up? Stop recording.

HER: What was it that made you so scared of intimacy with your children?

HELEN: I wasn't at all. What are you? I've always held you.

HER: Hold me.

HELEN: What?

HER: Hold me now.

HELEN: Oh come don't be ridiculous.

HER: Hold me now.

HELEN: Well I've got no reason to do I?

HER: I'm your daughter.

HELEN: That isn't a reason.

HER: Why not? Mothers hold their daughters.

HELEN: You're thirty-five years old.

HER: I want to hold you.

HELEN: Okay fine. Here. Come on then. Otherwise you'll write some bloody article about how your mother didn't want to hug you and then all my colleagues will be bringing it up at academic board meetings and sniggering.

She hugs her.

HELEN: There. Is that?

HER: You want to stop?

HELEN: No. I'm perfectly happy to… Okay, yes let's. Very good. There you go. Intimacy.

HER: Congratulations.

HELEN: What does that mean?

HER: You look like you just went bungee jumping.

HELEN: Okay stop it now. Leave your poor mother alone. You sure you're not hungry?

HER: Why did you want to have another child after Mary? If you hated it so much.

HELEN: Oh no. I didn't. I wanted to kill myself when I found out I was pregnant with you. I mean life had been such an adventure until children. Well you know the stories from the sixties. And it really was. It was a riot. I mean we lived in Kashmir for three years on a –

HER: On a houseboat I know.

HELEN: That was the happiest time.

HER: You wanted to kill yourself?

HELEN: Oh yes.

HER: Thanks Mum.

HELEN: Don't get me wrong. It's been very entertaining watching your life. Especially your twenties. They were hilarious. But I could have done without it too. Your Dad stopped being as fearless. Was always worried about one of you getting sick or run over. That was a disappointment. I always loved how reckless he was.

HER: Then why didn't you use contraception?

HELEN: Oh I did. But I was always very forgetful with it. I mean maybe that's the key for you and your, I'm not allowed to call it an issue can I?

HER: Mum.

HELEN: Maybe you just need to take the pressure off. Maybe the moment you stop worrying…

1.7

MARY: Any problems?

HER: No. No he was perfect.

MARY: Little bastard.

HER: Hey.

MARY: You're always showing off around her, aren't you? Sleeping and laughing and cuddling calmly. You save the night-long tantrums and explosive shits for me, don't you? He's waging a war of attrition, this little fucker.

HER: Hey, he can hear you.

MARY: He's asleep. For once.

HER: They can feel the negative energy anyway.

MARY: I don't mean it. Not really.

HER: Yes you do.

MARY: Is it bad that I imagine strangling him?

HER: Jesus.

MARY: I mean only at four in the morning. And I've given him everything. And he's still… I took him to the hospital the other day. We thought there must be something really bad and as soon as he got there he was smiling at all the nurses and I said I swear he wasn't like this at home and they ran all the tests and then when we got back in the car he started howling. I think he hates me.

HER: Mary.

MARY: I do, I think he has it in for me.

HER: I think you need a break.

MARY: I mean what's wrong with me? Look at you. With you he looks so –

HER: Yeah?

MARY: Totally. Oh my fucking God.

HER: Really?

MARY: Like he could sleep forever. It's a miracle. Do you want him?

HER: What?

MARY: Take him. You can have him. I'm joking.

HER: Mary…

MARY: I'm not joking.

HER: What about David?

MARY: What about David? He doesn't give a shit. He sleeps through the whole thing.

HER: Why don't you wake him up?

MARY: I try to but he grumbles and then we fight it's just easier if do it myself. Seriously. Take him. David won't even notice. He's too busy on the playstation.

HER: Playstation?

MARY: Yeah it's much better since I bought him a playstation. He never goes out anymore.

HER: Oh my God.

MARY: And whenever he gets stuck on a level he'll do something for me to let out the frustration. He even cooked me a steak the other night. He hadn't used the barbecue since we got married.

HER: Mary, why don't you just leave?

MARY: Because I'm scared of being alone aren't I? And I've seen what happens to all the other women my age. Everyone tells them to get out, get out, he's no good for you, where's your self-respect, there's so many fish in the sea, and then they do, and there's no fucking fish in the sea, except like the ancient inedible ones, like pufferfish or whatever.

HER: The Japanese eat pufferfish. It's a delicacy. You just need to know how to cut around the poison.

MARY: I don't want to cut around the poison. I want to go to Tesco and buy two filleted fish...fuck this metaphor.

HER: You started it.

MARY: No I'm sticking with what I know. I mean what else is out there for me? Ex-rapists and birdwatchers. And it's not killing me, is it? The only thing that might is this little fucker here.

HER: Hey.

MARY: I know. I'm a terrible mother. I'm a very unmotherly mother. Maybe it is an idea? You taking him?

HER: Stop this.

MARY: I'm serious. I'm wearing thin here. I'm all frayed ends.

HER: Go see a psychologist.

MARY: We could do a trial. See how we both go?

HER: You are serious aren't you?

MARY: Why not?

HER: Is that why you keep bringing him around?

MARY: I'm fucking depressed.

HER: No.

MARY: I stand on the tube platform and dare myself to jump.

HER: NO. Stop this NOW. You're going to get yourself some therapy and I'm going to get myself pregnant. We both have perfectly normal perfectly common problems and there are solutions.

MARY: It's been two years love.

HER: I KNOW IT'S BEEN TWO YEARS. Here look. I have a fucking calendar. You think you need to remind me?

MARY: Where's John gone?

HER: He forgot his hard-drive or whatever at the office. He needs it for the meeting in Tel Aviv.

MARY: He's going to Tel Aviv?

HER: Yes he's going to Tel Aviv.

MARY: When?

HER: Tomorrow morning.

MARY: Didn't he just get in on Friday?

HER: Yes. He just got in on Friday.

MARY: Oh darling.

HER: Don't. It's fine. We're fine. No. Don't look at me like that. It's all okay. He's coming back Wednesday.

MARY: Wednesday? Okay.

HER: He's coming back Wednesday.

MARY: What time? You want to have dinner?

HER: No. He knows it's my birthday. He'll be back.

MARY: Alright. I won't make any plans. So just call.

HER: He's. Coming. Back.

MARY: Alright.

HER: Alright.

MARY: You know, darling, two years of unprotected sex…

HER: I know. I know.

MARY: It might be him, you know. If your gynaecologist says there doesn't seem to be anything wrong then, well, it might be –

HER: I know. He won't get it tested.

MARY: What? Why not?

HER: Wounded pride I guess.

MARY: Fucking men.

HER: And he's very busy.

MARY: Jesus.

HER: What?

MARY: You sound like…

HER: What?

MARY: You never sounded like that before.

HER: Sound like what?

MARY: It always gave me hope. That one of the two of us…

HER: Sound like what?

MARY: Like me when I'm defending David.

…

MARY: You're getting angry now.

…

MARY: Hello?

HER: John is *there* for me.

MARY: It's very fucking hard to be there for you when he's on another continent.

HER: And John has never. He would never.

MARY: Okay that's not what I meant but okay.

HER: So the comparison is frankly –

MARY: You're angry, let's change the topic.

HER: Oh great. Good. Let's change the topic. You sound like John. Let's change the topic. Let's change the topic.

…

...

MARY: Are you alright?

HER: I'm fine. I said I was fine. I'm fine.

1.8

HER: Oh –

JOHN: Hi.

VICTOR: Hello.

JOHN: Hi.

HER: What are you –

JOHN: I went home and well you weren't –

HER: What I thought your flight got in at midnight?

JOHN: It did.

HER: What time is it?

JOHN: Three.

HER: Oh.

JOHN: Yeah oh.

HER: Do you remember –

JOHN: Yeah. Yeah I do. Hi again.

VICTOR: Hi again.

JOHN: I didn't realise you were back in the –

HER: Yes you do I told you I emailed you.

JOHN: I don't think so.

HER: I whatsapped you or something.

JOHN: Welcome back.

VICTOR: Thanks.

HER: I did tell you.

JOHN: Working late?

VICTOR: Yeah it's this whole Brexit thing.

JOHN: You guys really fucked up there didn't you?

HER: Excuse me?

VICTOR: Brexit.

HER: Oh yeah. Right. Is it really three in the morning?

JOHN: Almost quarter past.

HER: You must be knackered.

JOHN: Getting there.

HER: Sorry love. We got a bit side-tracked. We were. It's the funniest. You tell him.

VICTOR: What?

HER: The thing about the –

VICTOR: Oh yeah.

HER: Tell him.

JOHN: I'm actually really quite tired.

HER: No. No. Listen to this. It's so funny.

VICTOR: I don't think it will work in the retelling.

HER: No go on.

VICTOR: It's about Marilyn and the happy birthday song. It's just a stupid gag…

JOHN: The birthday…

HER: Uh huh.

VICTOR: I told it back to front and somehow it made it funnier.

JOHN: Shit.

VICTOR: And then we just got on a riff with misremembered jokes, it was…

JOHN: It's Wednesday isn't it?

HER: Thursday now. Almost quarter past three in the morning.

JOHN: Fuck. I'm… I totally knew. I totally planned to…

HER: You had no choice. The meeting went over.

JOHN: I'm really sorry.

HER: They always go over.

JOHN: You've been… That's why there's a…

HER: Yeah we got one from Marks and Sparks. But I convinced Victor only one candle. Don't need a suicide on our hands do we?

JOHN: I'm sorry honey.

HER: Now we both are.

VICTOR: I think I should probably get –

HER: NO. No. You're staying right here. Let's get drunk. I'm already drunk. Let's get more drunk.

VICTOR: I've got Tess tomorrow.

HER: What? You've got a test tomorrow? Like an exam? What for?

VICTOR: Tess. My daughter.

HER: He has a daughter.

JOHN: I just heard.

HER: He wasn't even really with the woman. She was a lapsed Seventh Day Adventist but then she unlapsed. Or relapsed. Or something. Crazy world huh? Where's the champagne? I got a bottle of Dom from the supermarket. The supermarkets around here are so posh.

JOHN: How old's your – ?

VICTOR: Almost four.

JOHN: Great age.

VICTOR: Yeah.

HER: What the fuck would you know?

JOHN: What?

HER: About four-year-olds? "Great age." What the fuck does that even mean?

JOHN: I guess you're right.

HER: CRRRAZY FUCKING WORLD yeah we just got to talking about misremembered jokes and misremembered pasts and regrets and the snaky fucking paths life takes you know, the insidious venomous slither of life, and I thought fuck it, I'd have a drink, we only bought one bottle though, that's kindergarten shit, remember me in the old days John? Remember me in the old days Victor?

JOHN: Yes I do.

HER: Victor? Say yes I do.

…

HER: VICTOR.

VICTOR: Sorry, man.

JOHN: That's alright.

HER: See, Victor? It's alright. Go on. Say it. Do you remember me in the old days?

VICTOR: Yes. I do.

HER: That's the problem. The memory. It's always the fucking problem. You can't scrub it away.

JOHN: Hey maybe we should –

HER: The Old Days. Who would have fucking thought?

2.9

JOHN: How you feeling?

HER: I'm great. Shall we go home?

JOHN: We are home.

HER: I know that was a joke.

JOHN: Haha.

HER: Most losers have to go home after their wedding night.
Not us. We totally rule. Our honeymoon is us both being in the same place at once and that place being our home. For at least three days.

JOHN: Five.

HER: I bet you'll be on a plane in three.

JOHN: How much.

HER: Five blowjobs.

JOHN: Deal.

HER: I'm totally going to win and then you'll be going down to pussy town ALL month.

JOHN: My pleasure.

HER: Is it?

JOHN: Don't start that.

HER: I'm not. I'm going to be a good wife. Good ole wifey.

JOHN: You drunk?

HER: You know I'm not.

JOHN: You're lying on the ground.

HER: I'm enjoying our backgarden. You know I don't think I've been out here since we bought the place.

JOHN: Yes you have I saw you smoking out here several times.

HER: That doesn't count. The midnight fag doesn't count. I mean in a holistic sense. A woman and her garden. Herbs.

JOHN: You want herbs?

HER: Vegetables. Sunflowers. Chilli plants. Geraniums. Maybe not geraniums. I'm going to start gardening.

JOHN: Okay. Good idea. Will you write a blog about it?

HER: Is that a dig?

JOHN: It was a joke.

HER: Does my blog bother you? I'm not using your name.

JOHN: Your Wikipedia page links to mine.

HER: Yeah but there's plausible deniability. I could be fictionalising the whole thing.

JOHN: I'm sure that's what everyone thinks.

HER: Hey husband.

JOHN: Hey wife.

HER: We are such fucking clichés.

JOHN: We are.

HER: Why did we do this again?

JOHN: You needed a change.

HER: Is that why? Is that? Why?

JOHN: And besides I've never had such an issue with the idea. I've kind of fantasised about it.

HER: Did your fantasies look like this? A middle aged woman with her skirt up around her thighs making love to a patch of grass?

JOHN: Quarter aged at most. They didn't look *unlike* this.

HER: What did you imagine?

JOHN: I imagined it earlier. Calmer.

HER: I am calm. Calm as fuck.

JOHN: You are. You're wonderful.

HER: Thank you hon so are you.

JOHN: I imagined something slightly more traditional and maybe a few more friends.

HER: We have no friends.

JOHN: We used to.

HER: We used to have a life.

JOHN: Now we have each other.

HER: And my empty womb.

JOHN: I love you. And please never say that again. We're just at the beginning.

HER: Oh come on. We're at least in the middle. If not the beginning of the end.

JOHN: There's so much time still. There is. No panic.

HER: No panic. Just champagne.

JOHN: Now you're talking.

HER: Not for me.

JOHN: You chose a great time to quit. You might be the only the only sober bride this side of the twentieth century.

HER: Oh I don't know. I'm sure there's been plenty of sober pregnant brides. I'm just getting my body ready to join the club.

JOHN: Speaking of.

HER: Yes?

JOHN: I think I should…

HER: What?

JOHN: Mary's pregnant again and she's too scared to tell you.

HER: Oh. Again.

JOHN: Yeah.

HER: That's –

JOHN: Yeah.

HER: That's great news. Good juju.

JOHN: She thought you'd be upset.

HER: I'm not I'm excited. It's a good omen. Want to stumble upstairs?

JOHN: Gladly.

HER: Who's going clean up this dump? I have to start gardening tomorrow.

JOHN: Your mum, your sister and Victor are already at it.

HER: Victor's lovely.

JOHN: He is.

HER: My hand feels heavy.

JOHN: Huh?

HER: This ring. It really makes my hand feel heavy.

JOHN: Is that a metaphor?

HER: No. I like it. Like every time I lift it to do something I'll remember you.

JOHN: You'll get used to it.

HER: Yeah I probably will. Shame. I'm going to put tomatoes over there. That gets sun most of the day.

JOHN: How do you know?

HER: I have no fucking clue. I've always wanted a fig tree.
I'm going to start jogging. There's that National Trust place round the corner. I'm going to jog around that.

JOHN: It's like it's new year. All these resolutions.

HER: Ten new years in one. A thousand new beginnings. Give me a kiss.

They kiss.

HER: When I imagine our child I imagine it's a boy. With that cheeky look of yours like what's going on inside his mind is much much naughtier than he would ever let out. But when he gets scared he has to come here. Here against my thigh, and burrow in. Close his eyes and pretend the world doesn't exist and all he hears is my voice saying it's okay it's okay.

…

HER: Is it?

JOHN: What honey?

HER: Is it okay?

JOHN: Of course it is.

2.10

MARY: What are you doing?

HER: What does it look like I'm doing?

MARY: Do you even know how to do that?

HER: Yeah I watched a YouTube tutorial. Try saying that five times really fast.

MARY: YouTube tut – no. I always just get a man in.

HER: I want to garden. Grow things. Watch them grow. Nurture them.

MARY: Yeah I've got the picture.

HER: What's up with you?

MARY: I um…

HER: What? What is it darling?

MARY: I can't…um…

HER: Hey. Hey. It's okay.

…

HER: Did he cheat on you again?

MARY: No. No. It's…

HER: What?

MARY: I lost the baby.

HER: Oh. Darling.

2.11

DES: Now we're talking. Now we're cooking with gas. We are cooking with weapons grade plutonium. This is next level shit. Fuck. Yes. Fuck yes. Are you happy?

HER: Huh?

DES: 3000 hits in the last twenty minutes. This shit is *viral* baby. We're going to be trending in a second. I've had friends texting me. Is that your boss? I'm like shit yeah, she's *the* boss.

HER: Stop it.

DES: This bit, jesus, "when I heard her baby had died, waves of relief poured through me, my face showed sympathy, sisterly love, but every part of me breathed a sigh of secret satisfaction." BOOM

HER: It's not, don't do that –

DES: And this "I sat with her in the hospital as she prepared to give birth to her dead child, holding her reassuringly, whispering it's okay, and wondering had I done this? I'd wished for this so many times, in the darker moments, hoping for some kind of level playing field, like a spinster with a voodoo doll – "

HER: Okay. That'll do. Mary's never going to talk to me again.

DES: She'll get over it. It's a confessional. People understand that. People totally want that. You think no one else has ever had these thoughts? I mean Al Gore.

HER: Al Gore.

DES: No. That's not it. He was the environmentalist almost president.

HER: What are you talking about?

DES: Gore Vidal. "Every time a friend succeeds something in me dies." You see?

HER: I see that I've joined the ranks of the narcissists.

DES: You. Are the fucking. Zeitgeist baby. The fucking zeitgeist. People are lapping this shit up.

HER: People always lap nastiness up.

DES: NO. No. Confession. Catharsis. The unrepresented millions. The dark secret brought into the light. This is journalism. This is exposé. You're brilliant.

HER: Thanks.

DES: Don't back off. Or I'll beat the shit out of you. And you know I could.

2.12

JOHN: Will you come inside?

HER: Sorry?

JOHN: I want to talk to you will you come inside?

HER: Am I in trouble?

JOHN: Don't. What is that? You're not twelve.

HER: Sorry boss.

JOHN: What are you doing?

HER: I'm joking. What are you doing?

JOHN: Do you want to tell me something?

HER: Tell you what?

JOHN: I don't want to have this conversation outside.

HER: What, are you going to shout at me?

JOHN: What is your problem?

HER: What is your problem?

JOHN: Okay, I'm just going to –

HER: What? Get on another plane? Organise a meeting in Taipei?

JOHN: My friends read what you write. You know that don't you?

HER: Oh right so this is what it's about.

JOHN: My colleagues. My clients. I mean do you even consider the –

HER: I'm not using your name.

JOHN: They know I'm your fucking husband. They always have. There are photos of us together on the internet. And you can say whatever you like about yourself, I mean it's embarrassing, but it's your own life –

HER: You're embarrassed by me?

JOHN: But when you start fucking talking about erectile dysfunction which you know it wasn't –

HER: Oh come on it was a speculation.

JOHN: You know how fucking drunk I was that night, I can barely even remember getting home and there is no fucking way I would have, could have initiated sex, so when you start writing nasty dissections of my flaccid fucking –

HER: No there's no way you would *ever* initiate sex.

JOHN: My *willingly* flaccid penis. The penis of an unconscious man, as if there were some kind of failure in it not –

HER: It was a condemnation of myself. Of me. That I felt the need to – that I've lost all sense of self-respect.

JOHN: You know what? I am embarrassed. You embarrass me.

HER: Fuck you.

JOHN: I don't care how shit this gets. I mean I can deal with how shit this is getting.

HER: What's that supposed to mean?

JOHN: Us. I can deal with the fucking *cracks* in us. I can deal with not knowing what version of the woman I used to know I'm coming home to –

HER: If you *ever do* –

JOHN: What I cannot deal with is the fucking world laughing behind my back.

HER: I had *three* days I could have got pregnant, you were supposed to be back for all of them, you were back for *one*, you met your friends for a fucking boozer –

JOHN: It was my best friend's stag party –

HER: You spend the night with strippers instead of me, you get home at three, listen to me –

JOHN: There weren't any strippers, Jesus you're –

HER: You get home at three, fall unconscious, what am I supposed to do? I've been fucking sitting up waiting because you *promised* –

JOHN: That's life. Things like that happen.

HER: So yeah, I fucking *try*, I humiliate myself, going down on my unconscious husband, trying to get what you promised me I could –

JOHN: Jesus are you hearing yourself? I'm not a fucking cow. You can't just fucking milk me.

HER: You promised things would be different.

JOHN: And you promised you would stop obsessing about this shit you promised to give me a break from all this fucking you promised me a fucking moratorium on this –

HER: I CAN'T my body is not letting me I can't I can't let this go I can't.

JOHN: Alright. Alright. Now all the neighbours know about it. If they haven't already read about it.

HER: You aren't in here.

JOHN: No I'm not.

HER: You're not getting the messages I'm getting. Every single second of every single day.

JOHN: No I get other messages. I have messages too. And I ignore them. I mean if we were all just our fucking biology then we might as well just go back to knocking women over the head with clubs and dragging them back to our –

HER: I want to listen to them. I want to want what they're telling me to want. And I want you to want it too.

JOHN: I do.

HER: Do you?

JOHN: Of course I do.

HER: Look at me. Look at me when you say it. Do you want it John? Because I need to know.

JOHN: Yes. I want it too.

HER: Say it. Say the actual.

JOHN: I want to have a child. With you.

HER: I need you to stop travelling so much.

JOHN: It's not a good time for me to –

HER: I need that.

JOHN: Okay.

HER: I need you to get your sperm tested. The doctors won't do any more tests on me until they get your results.

JOHN: Okay.

HER: Okay?

JOHN: Okay.

HER: I made you an appointment for Tuesday.

JOHN: Actually, I'm supposed to be –

HER: John.

JOHN: Okay.

HER: Good. Thank you.

JOHN: I need something from you.

HER: Yeah? Of course.

JOHN: I need you to stop writing about it.

…

JOHN: Hm?

HER: I can't do that.

JOHN: Oh. Jesus fucking Christ. Jesus fucking Christ. Jesus fucking Christ.

2.13

HER: Thanks. Thanks.

VICTOR: What's up? Are you okay?

HER: I'm... Sorry I'm...

VICTOR: Hey...

HER: John's gone.

VICTOR: Okay, he's...

HER: He's disappeared.

VICTOR: What do you mean? Where is he?

HER: That's exactly it. I have no – His phone's not –

VICTOR: Okay slow down. What happened.

HER: Two days ago. We had an argument.

VICTOR: Right.

HER: He never does this.

VICTOR: You want to go to the police?

HER: Oh no. God no. He won't have. No. His career's going too well.

VICTOR: Okay well.

HER: What am I supposed to do?

VICTOR: Are you sure his phone's off?

HER: Yeah it's going to answer machine.

VICTOR: Yeah but maybe's –

HER: What?

VICTOR: How angry was he? He might have blocked you.

HER: What? What's that?

VICTOR: You can block a contact. And it goes straight to answer machine.

HER: Oh.

VICTOR: If you gave me his number I could see if it goes through with me.

HER: Oh. Should we?

VICTOR: Well at least you'd know he's not...

HER: Okay. Here.

VICTOR: Okay...

HER: Do I smell?

VICTOR: What no.

HER: I haven't showered in two days. I've been trying to sleep through it.

VICTOR: No. No. You smell good.

HER: Good? Hey.

VICTOR: I mean fine. You smell totally... Oh shit.

He hangs up.

HER: What? What was that?

VICTOR: He answered.

HER: That fucker.

VICTOR: Oh shit.

HER: That fucking fucker.

VICTOR: I think he heard me say "you smell totally..." Oh shit. That's. Shit.

HER: I can't believe that.

VICTOR: I'm sorry.

HER: No. Him. I mean I would never...

VICTOR: Well, he's alive.

HER: Not for long.

VICTOR: What was your argument about?

HER: Oh well...

VICTOR: Sorry that's none of my business.

HER: No. No. You know. The usual.

VICTOR: The what?

HER: You've read the...

VICTOR: No. I haven't. It's not really my kind of –

HER: Oh.

VICTOR: Sorry.

HER: You never read the bit I wrote about you?

VICTOR: What bit?

HER: Oh. Nevermind.

VICTOR: What? What did you write about me?

HER: Nevermind.

VICTOR: Why are you smiling?

HER: Victor...

VICTOR: I'm going to go online now and –

HER: NO. Don't. That's embarrassing.

VICTOR: What did you?

HER: Please don't.

VICTOR: What was it?

HER: I used a pseudonym.

VICTOR: Because it's so bad?

HER: Quite the opposite.

VICTOR: Shit. This is. Okay. I should go home.

HER: No. No. Stay. I can't sleep. The tree at the front keeps scratching against the window.

VICTOR: You want me to cut it back for you?

HER: I haven't got a ladder.

VICTOR: I could see if I could climb up and –

HER: Victor. Please. Just stay.

VICTOR: Okay.

HER: Okay?

VICTOR: No.

HER: No?

VICTOR: No that was like an "okay look" okay. That was the beginning of a sentence.

HER: Okay.

VICTOR: Look.

HER: Okay.

VICTOR: I've got a… I've just started seeing someone.

HER: Oh. How's that going?

VICTOR: Yeah, it's… It's good, it's comfortable.

HER: Comfortable?

VICTOR: I mean yeah it's…and you and John will…patch things up I'm sure…

HER: I'm thirty-eight years old Victor. And nothing's happening. I've been trying for years and nothing's happening. And I keep thinking about back then. When we…

VICTOR: Oh.

HER: Maybe we should have kept it.

VICTOR: Oh God.

HER: I was an idiot.

VICTOR: You were twenty-three.

HER: That's a good age. That would have been a good age.

VICTOR: I know I tried to talk you out of it but you made the right decision. I was a stupid conservative young man. And you knew exactly what you were doing. That's what I meant. What I said four years ago. It was. Exactly that. That I'm sorry. That I even questioned your right to. And look at what you've done with your –

HER: Career?

VICTOR: Yes.

HER: I was told I could have both. They fucking lied to me.

VICTOR: No they didn't. You can. You will.

HER: I haven't got any time left.

VICTOR: Yes you do.

HER: Nothing like that ever happened with John. Not once. I've never had a mistaken…anything. And there hasn't been any contraception now for…well you know how long…

VICTOR: Sometimes it just…

HER: You and I … Well we know that we can…

VICTOR: Is that what? Is that why you?

HER: Why not?

VICTOR: Oh fuck.

HER: I need help.

VICTOR: I can't believe I'm. Oh my God.

HER: Victor.

VICTOR: I'm sorry I –

HER: Don't you fucking leave. Don't you dare fucking leave.

60

VICTOR: I'll see you at work okay?

2.14

HER: Pregnancy yoga is the bomb. My pelvic floor is like a fucking like a fucking…what's something that's flexible and muscly at the same time? It's like a fucking *octopus*. Pre-pregnancy yoga. Maybe-baby yoga. Ha.

MARY: Hey…

HER: You're going to start talking and then you're going to tell me how disappointed you are and that'll be so much more painful to take than anger because you're so above that aren't you?

MARY: No. I'm not. I am angry.

HER: But you've worked through it. It took a couple of months but now you're composed. And you've found a very high horse to ride in on.

MARY: I'm concerned. Actually. And angry as I might be that's –

HER: Santa Maria. My God. Have you actually ever thought about the underlying semantics of that? The *Virgin* Mary. You know how fucking poisonous the philosophy that lies at the heart of our entire culture is? I mean she's the role model isn't she? Isn't she?

MARY: I don't know.

HER: And she was a virgin. And God fucked her or whatever. No. No. That's the perverse interpretation. That God was a fucker. Please God, hear me, you are not a fucker. I've never… I mean if I've offended you in any way and that's why…then I'll do anything to make it up to you. I know you're not a fucker. No. God is all-capable, clicks his fingers, bang, baby. That's the conception we all aspire to. Immaculate fucking no problems oops I've never even seen a dick here we go let's give birth to the son of God. Which every woman essentially thinks they have done. Hard work? NO. Never even heard of sex and I'm already pregnant. I'm a having a low blood sugar moment.

MARY: Do you think you need to see someone?

HER: HA.

MARY: I'm serious.

HER: Don't you want to swear at me at least?

MARY: I don't know that I'd get any satisfaction out of it.

HER: I always get satisfaction out of swearing at people. Even geriatrics and small children. I hate small children. I don't really.

MARY: Don't you?

HER: What's that supposed to mean?

MARY: It was Freddie's birthday last weekend.

HER: Yeah I know.

MARY: I called you.

HER: Yeah I know.

MARY: He asked where you were.

HER: Did he? How does he even remember who I am? He hasn't seen me in almost a year.

MARY: Because I talk about you a lot.

HER: I could have blocked you.

MARY: What?

HER: Did you know that's a thing?

MARY: What?

HER: Blocking people. Blocking their contacts?

MARY: Yeah. I did.

HER: Yeah. It's a thing. It's a real fucking thing.

MARY: Why didn't you come to Freddie's party?

HER: I can't. I'm sorry. It's just. I'm not in a very receptive place at the moment.

MARY: Receptive to what?

HER: You know. The whole other people's children thing. It makes me want to take up cutting again.

MARY: You used to cut yourself?

HER: Oh. No. I guess I didn't. But it sounds very appealing at the moment.

MARY: What the hell are you doing?

HER: I just came home from yoga and I'm about to make myself a fertility friendly breakfast why do you keep asking me that?

MARY: Where's John?

HER: Who?

MARY: John. Your husband.

HER: He's on a meditation retreat. Or was it a knitting workshop?

MARY: Did you sleep with him?

HER: Who? John? Barely ever.

MARY: Victor.

HER: Did I? Hm. Good question.

MARY: Stop it. Stop making fun of everything.

HER: Sorry…

MARY: Are you trying to ruin your life?

HER: Or is my life trying to ruin me?

MARY: I think I'm going to call Mum.

HER: Oh yeah. Good idea. That trick always works.

MARY: I think we need to stage some kind of intervention.

HER: It's always a good plan to tell the intervenee first.

MARY: I'm worried about you.

HER: I think you're still angry. There wasn't any ill-will in what I wrote.

MARY: I know that darling.

HER: What am I saying? Of course there was. Gallons and gallons of it. But it wasn't directed at my sister per se. I mean not us as sisters.

I mean not at your womb specifically. Just at any womb that's full or getting fuller. My brain is doing some very strange things. Or is it my body? It's always so hard to tell.

MARY: I'm sorry.

HER: Why are you sorry Sis?

MARY: Because I didn't realise, I didn't notice things had gone this far.

2.15

JOHN: Fuck. Fuck. Fuck. Oh God. I'm sorry.

HER: Are you drunk?

JOHN: A little.

HER: It's four in the morning.

JOHN: I didn't mean to wake you. The fucking neighbour's dog won't stop barking. I was just going to slip in and then I realised I left my keys here. We used to have a spare key under the back door mat.

HER: I took it inside. There's been burglaries.

JOHN: Fuck this place used to be so ghetto. We never had to worry about burglaries.

HER: Are you smoking?

JOHN: No.

HER: What's that in your hand?

JOHN: A cigarette. I'm not smoking very much. I was just going to slip in and sleep on the couch so I could see you when you woke up. I didn't mean to wake you sorry hon.

HER: I'm not sleeping very well anyway.

JOHN: How you going?

HER: Shit. You?

JOHN: Really shit.

HER: What's wrong?

JOHN: We can talk about this in the morning. You should go to sleep.

HER: What is it John?

JOHN: Oh fuck.

HER: What?

JOHN: I really fucked up.

HER: What did you do?

JOHN: I spent the night with Kate. From the office. I didn't. I don't think we. I was really drunk. I don't know. I …

HER: Right.

JOHN: I think we just kissed and I fell asleep.

HER: Okay.

JOHN: I'm sorry hon. I'm sorry.

HER: Okay.

JOHN: Hon?

HER: I thought something like that was probably going to happen.

JOHN: Don't say that.

HER: Why did you come back?

JOHN: Because I don't want to, I don't want to…

HER: Lose me?

JOHN: I've been running away from you.

HER: I know.

JOHN: I left you on your own to deal with all the…

HER: Yeah.

JOHN: I've got this. Look.

HER: What's that?

JOHN: Look. I got my… I got it tested…

HER: Did you get an STD test at the same time?

JOHN: I didn't sleep with her. I woke up in my underpants. I still had my underpants on.

HER: And?

JOHN: Please hon, stop doing that with your voice, we can't, please…

HER: What does it say?

JOHN: I haven't read it yet. I was too scared.

HER: Of what?

JOHN: That you'd leave me if it was…or want to…you know… someone else…

HER: Well let's have a look.

JOHN: Can't we just go to sleep?

HER: No.

She opens it.

JOHN: What does it say?

2.16

JOHN: You should have whatever you need in the fridge. I stocked up last night.

HELEN: Okay thanks.

JOHN: The front door doesn't latch shut. You have to pull it hard. Like a loud hard slam.

HELEN: Okay good to know.

JOHN: Otherwise the cat gets out.

HELEN: Good to know.

JOHN: The cat's name is Leo.

HELEN: Obviously.

JOHN: Yeah right yeah.

HELEN: Goodo. That all seems to be –

JOHN: She likes avocado on toast for breakfast, with chilli oil. I've made up a batch of chilli oil, it's sitting on the counter next to the salt. You can do avocado on toast can't you?

HELEN: I've never been much of a cook.

JOHN: Just toast the toast and put a few chunks of avo on it. She can do the chilli oil herself.

HELEN: Okay.

JOHN: And the George Clooney machine is self-explanatory.

HELEN: Excuse me?

JOHN: The Nespresso machine. Clooney did the adverts.

HELEN: He was Batman wasn't he?

JOHN: Don't remind him of that.

HELEN: Sorry?

JOHN: Nevermind. I'll show you before I go. It's a capsule system.

HELEN: A what?

JOHN: You just put a capsule in and press the... I'll show you.

HELEN: Sure.

JOHN: Thanks for coming.

HELEN: Well it was very short notice.

JOHN: I appreciate it.

HELEN: It was very hard to find someone to take over my lectures.

JOHN: But you did?

HELEN: Sorry?

JOHN: Find someone.

HELEN: Well otherwise I wouldn't be here, would I?

JOHN: Well thanks, Helen.

HELEN: She's not talking?

JOHN: Oh no she talks, it's not like she's…

HELEN: Catatonic?

JOHN: No not catatonic. Well sometimes, sure, it can last a few hours, but it's not… It's the hormones she's on for the IVF.

HELEN: IVF?

JOHN: Yeah IVF.

HELEN: You guys are… Oh God…

JOHN: She didn't tell you?

HELEN: How long?

JOHN: We've done three rounds already.

HELEN: And?

JOHN: Well, we're still going. She didn't tell you?

HELEN: Not a word.

JOHN: Anyway the hormones are…

HELEN: Well of course they are, you know they induce a kind of menopause, to reboot the system so to speak?

JOHN: Yes, Helen, I do, I've been living with it.

HELEN: It's horrendous the lengths that women go to…

JOHN: Maybe don't say that to her.

HELEN: I mean she does know there are millions of orphaned children the world over, doesn't she?

JOHN: Definitely don't say that to her.

HELEN: Why not?

JOHN: She doesn't want to. She doesn't want to consider that right now. She still hasn't given up.

HELEN: She looks like she's given up.

JOHN: She's going to need. Um. A bit of positivity.

HELEN: Okay. I'll try. It's never been my strong suit I have to say.

JOHN: What?

HELEN: Positivity.

JOHN: Right.

HELEN: But I'll try.

JOHN: I'll be back in two weeks. I emailed you the itinerary.

HELEN: Yes I got it.

JOHN: Can you make sure she's awake to Skype with me every now and then? The time difference is a nightmare.

HELEN: Don't worry John. I'll handle it.

JOHN: The police came.

HELEN: Sorry?

JOHN: She'd been sitting opposite the playground down the road, watching the mothers with their children. She'd been there a lot, apparently. Pulled up in her car, just watching. The parents got freaked out.

HELEN: Oh.

JOHN: So we need to make sure she doesn't...

HELEN: Okay. Fine.

JOHN: And the cafe on the corner, there's a local mother's group that hangs out there on Tuesdays and Thursdays. So best to avoid that too.

HELEN: Well. I can see I won't have any time to read my stash of Scandinavian crime thrillers.

JOHN: I really need to make this trip.

HELEN: I'm sure you do.

JOHN: It's. They were threatening to pull the contract. I'd been trying to stay home as much as I can.

HELEN: It's okay John you don't need to explain.

JOHN: And we need all the money we can get right now.

HELEN: I thought it was you.

JOHN: You what?

HELEN: I thought you were the one with the...

JOHN: No. No.

HELEN: Oh. Well. Maybe the two of you are just not compatible.

JOHN: Helen.

HELEN: I'm not trying to be offensive.

JOHN: There were no eggs the first time we collected. The second time there were four. The third time just two. None of them were ever successfully fertilised. The chances even under optimal conditions are fifteen percent. I give my own sample every time. And there's always been plenty of healthy...

HELEN: Sperm.

JOHN: Yep. I don't know whether the question of compatibility even comes into it.

HELEN: How much longer are you going to...?

JOHN: That's up to her I guess.

2.17

HER: I can't even grow a tree.

VICTOR: Aren't you cold?

HER: I don't feel it anymore.

VICTOR: Do you want me to get you a coat?

HER: Says the man standing around in lycra.

VICTOR: I just cycled twenty miles.

HER: Want a coffee?

VICTOR: No, I should get going soon.

HER: Oh. Okay.

VICTOR: I. Um. Haven't seen you much at work.

HER: I've been doing more from home.

VICTOR: Des told me about the…

HER: Oh yeah.

VICTOR: How's that going?

HER: It's…going.

VICTOR: Right. Listen. I should. I'm leaving.

HER: Okay bye.

VICTOR: No. I mean. The paper.

HER: Oh.

VICTOR: I got a job in Hong Kong.

HER: Oh.

VICTOR: Yeah senior editor.

HER: Oh. Congratulations.

VICTOR: Me and Tess and Sophie, we'll be…

HER: Sophie?

VICTOR: My girlfriend.

HER: Girlfriend.

VICTOR: I told you about her back when…

HER: Sophie.

VICTOR: Yeah.

HER: How is that?

VICTOR: It's good. It's great.

HER: Is she?

VICTOR: What?

HER: You know.

VICTOR: Oh.

HER: She is. Isn't she?

VICTOR: Look...

HER: I can see it in your eyes.

VICTOR: I didn't want to...

HER: Congratulations.

VICTOR: I'm sorry.

HER: Why God you should be excited.

VICTOR: I am.

HER: You should be.

VICTOR: Thank you. I really didn't want to –

HER: When are you...?

VICTOR: Tomorrow night.

HER: Oh.

VICTOR: I thought I might see you at work but –

HER: Yeah like I said.

VICTOR: But I didn't want to leave without –

HER: Well that's very –

VICTOR: So I rode over.

HER: Long way to come.

VICTOR: Yeah.

...

VICTOR: I'll have my, obviously, and Facebook, are you still on –

HER: No. I had to get off. Too many trolls.

VICTOR: That's disgusting.

HER: That's the world.

VICTOR: I think it's very brave that you've kept writing about it. It's important. That other women who...

72

HER: Yeah.

VICTOR: I'll send you my new number, maybe we could FaceTime.

HER: You'll be otherwise occupied in a few months.

VICTOR: Ha yeah. August is the due…

HER: August. Lovely.

…

…

VICTOR: I'm sorry that I –

HER: Go on. Get out of here.

VICTOR: Okay.

…

VICTOR: Hey.

HER: Hey yeah?

VICTOR: Look after yourself.

2.18

JOHN: Give it to me.

HER: No.

JOHN: Hon.

HER: No.

JOHN: Give it to me.

HER: How am I supposed to go shopping?

JOHN: You never even leave the house.

HER: I leave the house.

JOHN: To go to the clinic.

HER: What, are you going to start giving me an allowance? Leave me cash on the counter in the mornings? Is that what? A kept woman?

JOHN: I don't want to have to do this.

HER: Oh my God that's what men used to say before they beat their wives.

JOHN: Give me the fucking…give me the credit card.

HER: It's my money too.

JOHN: We have no fucking money. We have no money. We can't make the payments on the mortgage. My card got declined at the fucking supermarket yesterday.

HER: I'm sorry.

JOHN: We agreed. No more.

HER: There's a chance we could –

JOHN: We tried. TWELVE times. We tried. It's time to –

HER: NO. No.

JOHN: We need to consider the other options. I got in contact with an adoption agency and I think we –

HER: My arms would freeze, my arms would fall off before I hold another person's child NEVER say that to me again NEVER –

JOHN: Why won't you at least meet them and see how you feel before you completely rule out the –

HER: I can feel it. I know it'll work this time. I can feel it.

JOHN: What can you feel?

HER: This time is going to be. This time is –

JOHN: We're sixty thousand pounds in debt. Sixty. Thousand. Pounds. We're going to lose the fucking house please I'm begging please please please just stop. I don't know what else I can say. Just. Stop. This. Now. Just. STOP.

HER: Honey.

JOHN: I'm begging you.

HER: Hon. It's okay. Hon.

JOHN: I can't. I can't do this anymore.

HER: You used to want this with me.

JOHN: I have. Nothing. Left.

HER: We used to be a team.

JOHN: I'm not going to give any more sperm samples.

HER: Okay. We can use the frozen sperm.

JOHN: I'm going to withdraw my permission to use that.

…

JOHN: I'm sorry. But this has to stop.

HER: I'll get a donor.

…

HER: I will.

JOHN: Okay. This is that conversation.

HER: I'm serious John.

JOHN: This the conversation we won't be able to go back from.

HER: Don't try and blackmail me into –

JOHN: What happened to us? Huh? We used to be so laissez-faire about everything. Nothing could unsettle us. Your father died and we were a team through that. Your sister and everything that. When I lost my job and then you helped me start the company. Everything we had to –

HER: We could still be a team.

JOHN: We need a fucking roof over our heads to be a. They'll take my fucking offices away from me. They'll audit the company, they'll –

HER: That's the only thing you ever think about.

JOHN: The. ONLY. Thing. I ever think about. Is you.

HER: Then help me.

JOHN: This isn't helping you. This is killing you. I don't recognise you. I don't. This isn't the no bullshit, nothing-will-kill-me fuck-you-if-you're-not-onboard chick I fell in love with.

HER: Oh. Right.

JOHN: You're letting the rest of the world tell you what you should believe in. This is other peoples' dream. This isn't our dream.

HER: It is. My dream.

JOHN: It never was.

HER: When wasn't it?

JOHN: Before. When it was us. You remember that? When it was really. Us.

HER: We were running away. You said so yourself.

JOHN: No. That started later. After this whole.

HER: This is me. This is me.

JOHN: We've ended up just like every bloody bourgeois cliche we promised we never would be. And what if we did end up getting pregnant? Are we going to be the couple pushing the twins down the street in the bugaboo to get a couple of flat whites in Primrose Hill?

HER: Wanting to have a child is not giving in.

JOHN: It is when the world. Is telling us. We can't.

HER: Fuck you.

JOHN: Okay. We can talk about this again tomorrow.

HER: You want my credit card. Here. And the other one. Here. And my fucking debit card. Take them. Take them.

JOHN: Thank you.

HER: Get that fucking smug look off your face.

JOHN: I'm trying to –

HER: Help me? You're killing me.

JOHN: When was the last time you saw the therapist?

HER: TUESDAY.

JOHN: I'm here for you.

HER: You're not. I look for you and I can't find you. You're not there anymore.

JOHN: I can't think of any other way to be there for you. I'm sorry. I'm trying.

HER: Okay. Fuck it. Fuck my stupid fucking cliche fucking. Fuck it. Let's get old and miserable. Let's do it.

JOHN: Don't say that.

HER: Let's get resentful and slink around each other's problems like ghosts and make tea and never talk and sit in the garden and slowly die let's leave nothing behind just the small insignificant marks someone will rub out as soon as we're gone. Let's. Be. Irrelevant.

JOHN: What's so wrong with that?

HER: That's it. That's a promise. I'll stop.

JOHN: Okay.

HER: I promise.

JOHN: Okay. Good. Thank you.

HER: Okay great.

JOHN: It'll get better. Soon. You'll see.

3.19

DES: What the hell are you doing?

HER: What? What's wrong? Get off me.

DES: Who was that guy?

HER: I'm fine. It's fine. Let go.

DES: You had his fucking…in your hand.

HER: Cock.

DES: Why are you…

HER: I thought that's what this whole thing was?

DES: I thought we were observing…

HER: Oh God don't be such a, I thought your generation was up for everything.

DES: Please, Boss, let's –

HER: Hey. Give me another…

DES: You've already had enough.

HER: GIMME. Gimme gimme GIMME.

DES: We're going to have to pump your stomach.

HER: Listen to me rookie. I'm a fucking pro at this. I was doing this when you were in nappies. Now give me another.

DES: Here.

HER: He was FIT.

DES: You can barely see straight.

… … … … … … …

JOHN: Mary are you okay?

MARY: Oh hi, John.

JOHN: What are you doing here?

MARY: Where is she?

JOHN: She's covering a festival.

MARY: What festival?

JOHN: I don't know. Some kind of. She barely talks to me anymore.

MARY: I went by her office. They gave me this.

JOHN: You went by her office?

MARY: I hadn't heard anything from her and she's never here when I call in. And then they said she'd been laid off.

JOHN: Laid… What?

MARY: You didn't know?

JOHN: She's writing for them this weekend.

MARY: I don't think so.

JOHN: She said it was an assignment.

MARY: They gave me her stuff to bring home. She never turned up to pick it up.

JOHN: Oh.

MARY: What's been going on between you two?

JOHN: I …

MARY: What?

JOHN: I don't know…

…………..

HER: You, who are you?

VICTOR 2: Who are you?

HER: You look like someone I know.

VICTOR 2: Oh yeah, who's that?

HER: Victor?

VICTOR 2: Okay, Victor, sure. You want to go somewhere?

HER: Where?

VICTOR 2: I have a tent on the other side of the field.

HER: We made a mistake Victor.

VICTOR 2: What mistake?

HER: Fucking Sophie. It was Sophie wasn't it?

VICTOR 2: Sophie who?

HER: Forget about Sophie. Come back. Come with me. Let's go to your place.

VICTOR 2: Okay.

HER: Which tube line is it on again?

VICTOR 2: You're funny.

....

JOHN: Hey. I just heard. Call me. Call me back. I need to talk to you. What are you doing? Where the hell are you? I don't even know where to come looking? Fucking hell. How did this happen? How did we grow so... Call me back. Send me a message. Anything.

....

HER: Who were you calling?

JOHN 2: My girlfriend. She's in Morocco.

HER: Why isn't she here?

JOHN 2: She's an anthropologist, she's studying the local –

HER: Shut up John, you can't fool me.

JOHN 2: Huh?

HER: Kiss me.

JOHN 2: Oh sorry. Like I said I've got a...

HER: Why don't you ever want to kiss me anymore?

JOHN 2: Okay, do you're very...

HER: KISS me.

JOHN 2: Sorry, I ...

HER: I want you inside me. I want all of you inside me. Every last drop. Is it raining?

JOHN 2: Oh. It has been for hours.

HER: Let's get wet.

JOHN 2: We are wet.

HER: Come on. Lie down with me.

JOHN 2: In the mud?

HER: John. You never were able to let go. Were you? You always wanted control. Didn't you?

JOHN 2: I'm just…

HER: JOHN.

JOHN 2: My name's Henry.

HER: Shut up John. I'll let you have control. I'll give in. Just don't tell anyone I let you… Here…

………………

MARY: Mum. Mum. Mum.

HELEN: What is it? What on earth are you…?

MARY: Don't you answer your phone?

HELEN: I had it on flight mode. I needed a break.

MARY: I think something's happened. I have a bad feeling. John can't find her. She hasn't called in days. She lost her job.

HELEN: Oh God.

MARY: Did she call you?

HELEN: No. No.

MARY: When did you last talk to her?

HELEN: Well to be honest I can't really remember… A while ago…

MARY: Jesus Christ.

………………

HELEN 2: What are you looking for?

HER: My child. I lost my boy.

HELEN 2: You brought your child to this…

HER: Yes. I've lost him somewhere here… In the field…

HELEN 2: Don't you think that's a little irresponsible?

HER: Like you can fucking talk Mum.

HELEN 2: Mum?

HER: Don't fucking lie to me. You left us at home. For hours. Wondering when you would… While you were doing fuck knows…

HELEN 2: Do you need any help love?

HER: I need to find my son. I lost him. A long time ago. And maybe he's cold and lost and…

HELEN 2: I'll call the ambulance. Do you remember what you've taken?

HER: Did you ever fucking care?

HELEN 2: Of course I care love, but I need a little help understanding –

HER: I treated my body like shit, I treated my life like it wasn't worth anything, because I never knew any different.

HELEN 2: Oh darling. I'm sure someone will have found him. Let's check at the lost and found tent.

… … … … … … …

JOHN: I'm calling you. You're not answering. I've been calling for hours. At least let me know you're alive. At least that. Show me at least that much respect. This is how you want to end it? Fuck. I really thought I knew you better than that.

… … … … … … …

HER: There you are.

VICTOR 2: Here I am.

HER: Where did you go?

VICTOR 2: Where did you go? I was looking for you.

HER: Really? Victor? I thought you were in Hong Kong?

VICTOR 2: You disappeared.

HER: I'm sorry. Fuck me. Fuck me right here.

VICTOR 2: There's people everywhere.

HER: We wasted so much time.

… … … … … … …

DES: Sorry can you, this is my friend. She needs to go home.

HER: Fuck off Des.

DES: Come on Boss. Let's go home. I ordered a car.

HER: You go home. I'm fine.

DES: You're not fine.

HER: I'M FINE. I'M FUCKING FINE.

VICTOR 2: Jesus Christ, I'm getting out of here.

HER: VICTOR.

VICTOR 2: She's a fucking crazy bitch. You need to get her some help.

DES: Why don't you fuck off you fucking cunt, yeah that's right get the FUCK OUT.

VICTOR 2: Crazy fucking bitches.

HER: Victor's always leaving.

DES: That wasn't Victor. You need some water. Here have some water.

She vomits.

DES: Oh shit.

HER: I'm okay I'm okay. Everything's okay.

3.20

JOHN: Oh. Hi.

HER: Were you asleep?

JOHN: Where have you been?

HER: Working.

JOHN: You lost your job.

…

JOHN: The removalists came yesterday. I got them to put the furniture in storage so we can separate it later.

HER: Separate it?

JOHN: Yeah. There's some things I'd like to keep but you can have most of it.

HER: Why are you…

JOHN: Obviously we'll have to talk about the proceeds from the house. You can use Graham as your lawyer, I'll find someone else.

HER: John.

JOHN: There's a leak as you can see… I've told the new owners. They're trying to get us to pay for it.

HER: Oh God. I can't have this conversation right now.

JOHN: I'd like to just get through this amicably and –

HER: John.

JOHN: Your dress is on back to front.

HER: What?

JOHN: Your dress. It's on back to front.

HER: What's that supposed to mean?

JOHN: I don't know. What is it supposed to mean?

HER: John, I'm going to go to sleep and then we can talk about this –

JOHN: There's no bed.

HER: I'll sleep on the floor. Like you did. I haven't slept for almost three days.

JOHN: I'm on a flight tomorrow morning. I'm going to stay in New York for a while.

HER: Okay fine. I'll see you when you get back.

JOHN: No. A while means a while. A long while.

HER: How long?

JOHN: I'm leaving.

HER: Everyone is.

JOHN: You're not understanding me.

HER: I understand what you're trying to say but I don't believe you John. You're just saying words to get a response. I'm sick of this game.

JOHN: Did you ever? Respect me?

HER: You never could stand not being the boss.

JOHN: Oh God.

HER: I need to *sleep*.

JOHN: Then sleep. And wake up when I'm gone.

HER: Okay.

JOHN: Just remember to leave the keys with Graham.

HER: Fine.

JOHN: Where will you stay?

HER: I don't know I don't fucking care.

JOHN: Okay. Well, good luck.

HER: Good luck to you.

…

HER: You never wanted a child with me, did you?

JOHN: I did.

HER: Not really. It never hurt you like it hurt me.

JOHN: It hurt me *because* it hurt you.

HER: Because you loved me. Which is not enough.

JOHN: How was that *not enough*?

HER: It never *hurt you*. *Your* dreams weren't being shattered. You watched my little obsession beat its head against a wall and you felt *pity*. You watched my fucking car crash like an innocent bystander and felt *sorry* for me –

JOHN: That's not. I was invested. Until you –

HER: *Invested?* Fuck off.

JOHN: You ate up all the fucking oxygen in our relationship. You left no room for me.

HER: I wanted you. To be on. My side.

JOHN: Sometimes that involves telling you when you've gone batshit fucking crazy in the nicest fucking way and expecting you to maybe listen and moderate your fucking, I can't do this, you're right, you go to sleep, I'll go to New York, our lawyers will –

HER: IF YOU WANTED A FUCKING CHILD THEN YOU WOULD HAVE MOURNED WITH ME you would have ached with me you would have hoped with me you would have STRUGGLED AND FUCKING FOUGHT AND NOT LET ANYTHING NOT LET ANYTHING NOT LET ANYTHING

JOHN: I wanted you.

HER: ME??

JOHN: YOU. TO BE HAPPY. YOU. TO BE MINE. I WANTED. You.

She laughs.

JOHN: And you let this unknown unpresent impossible fucking child get between us and you let it kill us you loved it like a new project because you always loved projects and you'd always been such a high-achiever and God forbid you didn't achieve this too but nature makes its own decisions and you let this hate start to fester between us the hate of me and the hate of my and the hate of your own and the only thing the only fucking thing you nurtured was this dead impossible dream that we both knew early on was dead and fucking fucking fucking gone the signs were there they were there you grew blind and obnoxious and stopped seeing me I was waiting for you to give up and come back just come back to the one who had always been waiting no conditions just you just me just us I was waiting for you and the hate grew of course it started growing in me too it did like a fucking tumour and it kept growing and I started wishing for the tests to come back negative for my sperm to be dead for your womb to be ruined for the eggs not to collect for the petri dish to be tainted for the seed not to catch for the end of this for the end of it because maybe then I could

86

get you back maybe then you'd wake up and see me then maybe we could –

HER: I fucking knew it.

…

HER: You didn't believe in it.

JOHN: No.

HER: This whole time you didn't believe in it.

JOHN: No.

HER: Get out of here. Get. The fuck. Out of here.

JOHN: I will.

HER: GET OUT GET OUT GET OUT I'LL FUCKING KILL YOU GET OUT.

3.21

HER: Oh shit I
John?
I think I
Oh

Oh
Okay
No more wondering
No more wondering
You won't be
Coming
You won't be coming anymore
My son
My daughter

But
Maybe
I'll be coming to you

I'll be coming
To you.